Microsoft®
Visual Studio LightSwitch
Help Website

Microsoft®
Most Valuable
Professional

Creating Web Pages
Using the LightSwitch HTML Client
in Visual Studio 2012

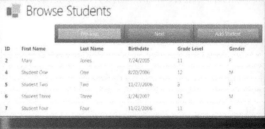

Michael Washington

Creating Web Pages
Using the
LightSwitch HTML Client
In Visual Studio 2012

Copyright 2013
Published By
The LightSwitch Help Website
http://LightSwitchHelpWebsite.com

Copyright

Table of Contents

Dedication

<u>Michael Washington</u>

As always, for Valerie and Zachary

Preface

Requirements

You must have Microsoft Visual Studio Professional 2012 (or higher) with HTML Client Preview 2 (or higher) to create the applications described in this book.

Thank You

<u>Microsoft:</u>

Andrew Lader
Beth Massi
Christopher Finlan
Dan Leeaphon
Eric Erhardt
Heinrich Wendel
Huy Nguyen
Jay Schmelzer
Joe Binder
John Rivard
John Stallo
Karol Zadora-Przylecki
Matt Sampson
Matt Thalman
Michael Eng
Michael Simons
Robert Green
Sheel Shah
Stephen Provine
Steve Anonsen
Steve Hoag

<u>LightSwitch Superstars:</u>

Alessandro Del Sole
Andrew Brust
Bill Quinn
Dan Beall
Delordson Kallon
Garth Henderson
Jan Van der Haegen

Jewel Lambert
John Juback
Kostas Christodoulou
Paul Patterson
Paul Van Bladel
Rich Dudley
Richard Waddell
Robert MacLean
Stephen J Naughton

Chapter 1: Understanding the LightSwitch HTML Client

This book covers using **Visual Studio LightSwitch 2012** to create HTML applications. The purpose of this book is to demonstrate its use, and to explain, and provide examples of important concepts of its API (Application Programming Interface).

What Is Visual Studio LightSwitch?

Visual Studio LightSwitch 2012 is a development tool that provides the easiest and fastest way to create *forms over data, line of business applications*.

It allows you to build applications for the desktop and the internet cloud. It does this by providing a tool that allows you to quickly and easily define and connect to your data, program your security and business rules, and expose this via OData to practically any 'client' such as mobile devices and web pages.

It allows you to create user interfaces using Silverlight and HTML. In this book we will only cover creating user interfaces using HTML.

The Visual Studio LightSwitch HTML Client

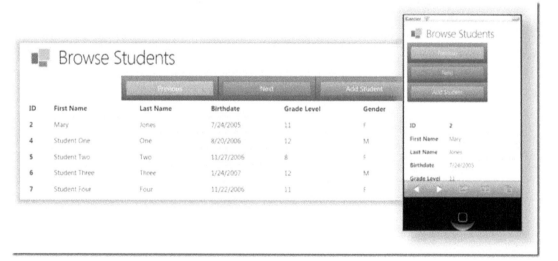

The purpose of the **LightSwitch HTML Client** is to create the HTML applications for the end user, whether they are using a mobile device or a desktop HTML web browser.

LightSwitch produces screens, which provide functionality that works well on both desktop and mobile web browsers.

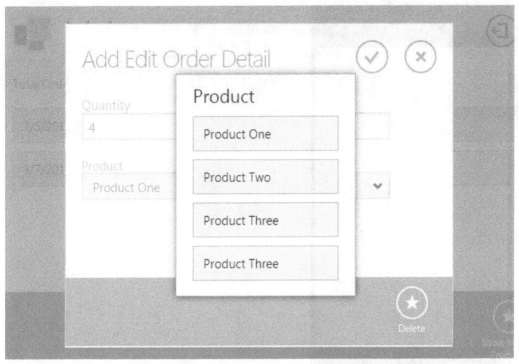

For example, a **LightSwitch** application allows the end users to click on a screen element and quickly display a popup that enables them to view details or edit data. In a desktop application, the end users will see the screen grayed out behind the popup. This lets the users easily track where they came from (and where they will return to).

If the user is using a tablet or a phone, the application will display only the popup; it will display the previous screen when he closes the popup.

This is important because we can create one application that works on all devices.

Single Page Application (because faster is better)

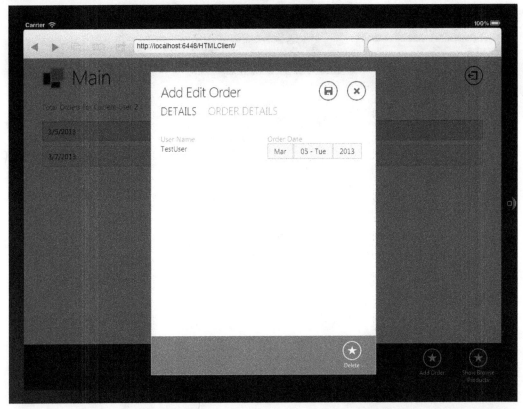

The **Visual Studio LightSwitch HTML Client** creates **Single Page Applications**. This design essentially means that when an end user arrives at your **LightSwitch** application, a thin **JavaScript** framework loads and it communicates with the back-end services using OData.

Most importantly, you don't have the slow *postbacks* that, while they are merely annoying on a desktop application, make the same application practically unusable on a mobile device (because they move so slowly due to being run on less powerful web browsers and slower internet connections).

Instead of *postbacks*, only the data is transferred back and forth when a user views and saves data. The screen is not redrawn each time. This makes for a much faster application.

Additional Features

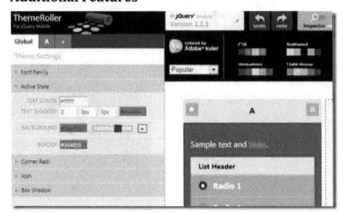

Every **LightSwitch** application does not have to *look like every other LightSwitch application.* You can use JavaScript plug-ins to create rich user interfaces.

You can also use **Themeroller** (http://jquerymobile.com/themeroller) to create custom themes for your **LightSwitch** applications.

Chapter 2: Create an End-To-End LightSwitch HTML Application

The sample code for this chapter can be obtained at the link "An End-To-End Visual Studio LightSwitch HTML5 Application" at http://lightswitchhelpwebsite.com/Downloads.aspx

In this chapter we will create an end-to-end **HTML** application in **Visual Studio LightSwitch**. The purpose is to demonstrate how **LightSwitch** allows you to create professional business applications that would take a developer many days to create. With **LightSwitch** you can create such applications in under an hour.

The Scenario

In this example, we will be tasked with producing an application that meets the following requirements for an order tracking system:

- Products
  - Add Products
  - Edit Products
  - Delete Products
- Orders
  - Add Orders
  - Edit Orders
    - Add Order Details
    - Edit Order Details
    - Delete Order Details
  - Delete Orders
- Business Rule
  - Allow the current user to only see his own orders
- Feature
  - Display the number of orders for the current user

Creating the Application

Open **Visual Studio** and select **File**, then **New Project**.

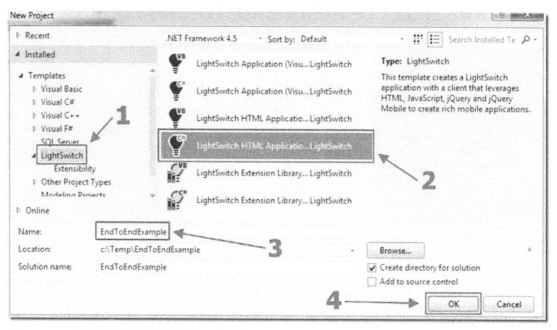

Create a new **LightSwitch HTML Application**.

*Note: You must have the **LightSwitch HTML Client** installed.*

The application will be created.

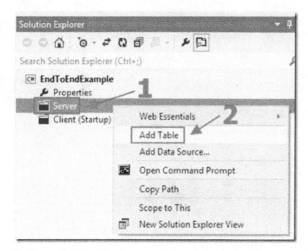

In the **Solution Explorer**, *right-click* on the **Server** node, and then select the **Add Table** option.

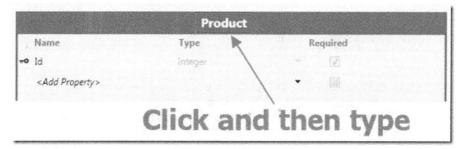

Click on the table name to edit it.

Change the table name to **Product**.

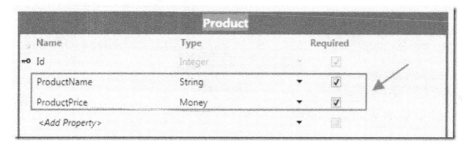

Add **ProductName** and **ProductPrice** fields to the table.

Click the **Save** button to save the table.

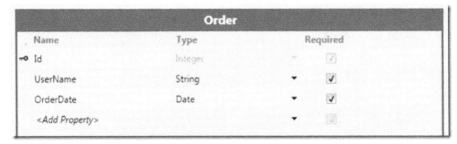

Create an **Order** table (with the fields in the image above).

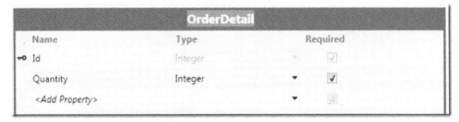

Create an **OrderDetail** table (with the fields in the image above).

Create Relationships

You will always want to make relationships in **LightSwitch** when you have tables that are related. This allows for optimal **LightSwitch** application construction. When creating queries, having relationships defined allows you to simply type a period to traverse from one entity to another. This saves a lot of coding work and reduces coding errors.

When creating user interfaces, defining relationships allows you to save a lot of coding work because **LightSwitch** will be able to automatically associate for example, **Order Details** with their associated **Order**.

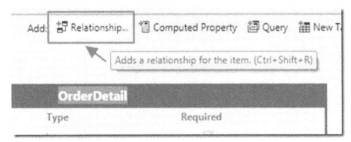

Click on the **Relationship** button to create a *relationship* between the **Order Detail** and the **Product** table.

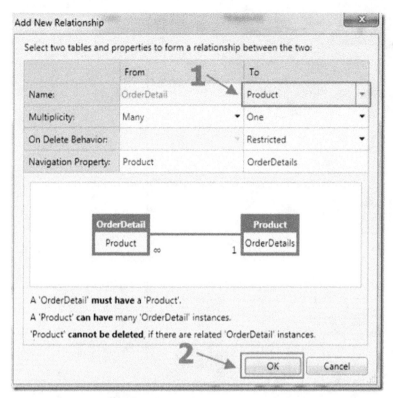

A box will appear. Select **Product** for the *"To"* table and click **OK** (ensure the other fields match the image above).

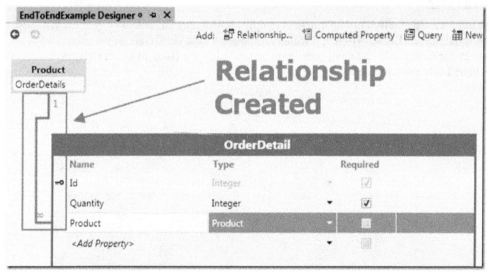

You will see that a relationship has been created. You can *double-click* on the line to edit the relationship.

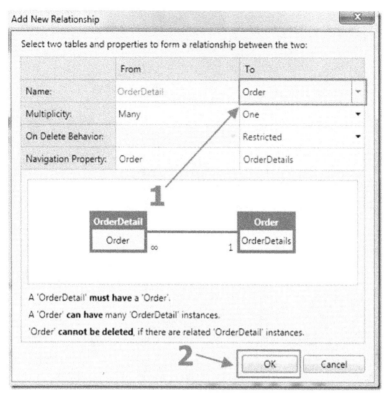

Click on the **Relationship** button again and make a new relationship to the **Order** table.

Create a Filter

One feature we are required to implement is to only show a user the orders he creates. We must keep in mind that all **LightSwitch** applications expose *all* data via OData so we must always set security in the server-side code, not only in the client-side code (such as the **HTML** or **Silverlight LightSwitch** client).

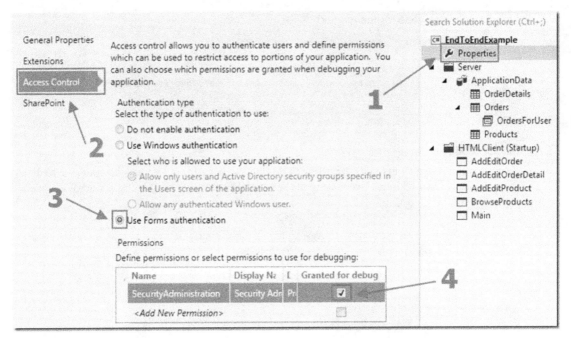

The first thing we need to do is turn on security. Click on **Properties**, then **Access Control** and then select **Use Forms authentication**. In addition, check the box next to **SecurityAdministration** to grant administration access to the **TestUser** account when you are debugging the application.

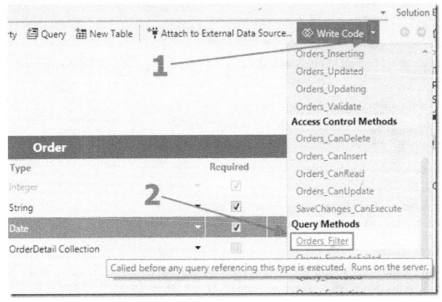

Next, we open the **Orders** table and select **Write Code**, then **Orders_Filter**.

Use the following code for the method:

```
partial void Orders_Filter(ref Expression<Func<Order, bool>> filter)
{
    // Only show the Orders for the current user
    filter = (x => x.UserName == this.Application.User.Identity.Name);
}
```

All data that accesses this table will pass through this filter.

Set Defaults

Keep in mind that we must set everything that relates to security in server-side code, we realize that marking orders with the **UserName** of the current user must be set using server-side code.

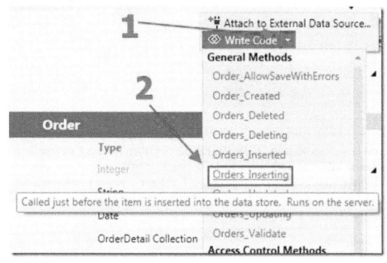

Open the **Orders** table and select **Write Code**, then **Orders_Inserting**. Use the following code for the method:

```
partial void Orders_Inserting(Order entity)
{
    // Set the Username
    entity.UserName = this.Application.User.Name;
}
```

Do the same for the **Orders_Updating** event.

Later, we will also set the **UserName** using client-side code; however, the server side code will always run and overwrite any value set client-side.

Create a Query

Another feature we are required to implement is to show the number of orders for the current user. We will make a query that we will later consume from the client-side.

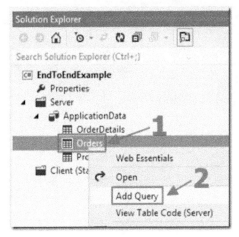

Right-click on the **Orders** table and select **Add Query**.

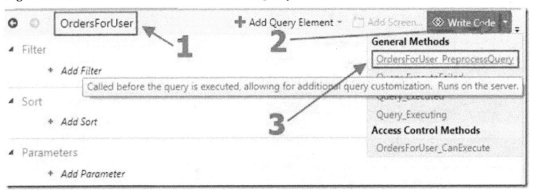

Name the query **OrdersForUser** by clicking on the title and editing it. Click the **Save** button to save the query. Next, click the arrow next to **Write Code** and then select **OrdersForUser_PreprocessQuery**.

Use the following code for the method:

```
partial void OrdersForUser_PreprocessQuery(ref IQueryable<Order> query)
{
    // Only show the Orders for the current user
    query = query.Where(x => x.UserName == this.Application.User.Identity.Name);
}
```

Create the User Interface For Products

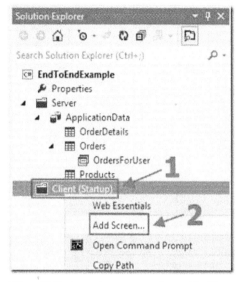

We will first create a screen that will allow us to see **Products**.

Right-click on the **Client** node in the **Solution Explorer** and select **Add Screen**.

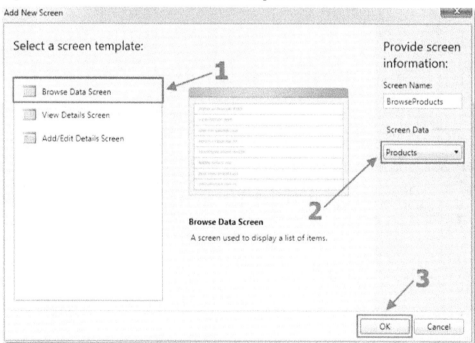

Create a **Browse Data Screen** using the **Products** table.

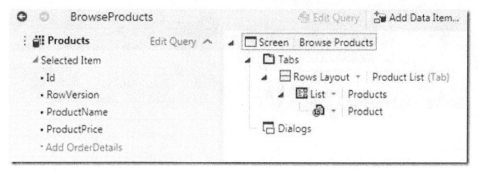

The screen will be created.

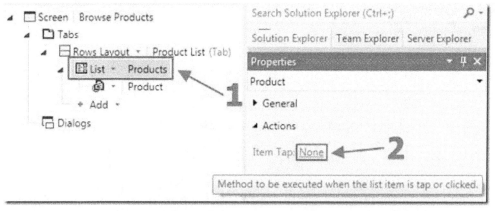

We will now create a screen that will allow us to edit a **Product** that is selected.

Click on the **Products List** and in its **Properties** select the **Item Tap** action.

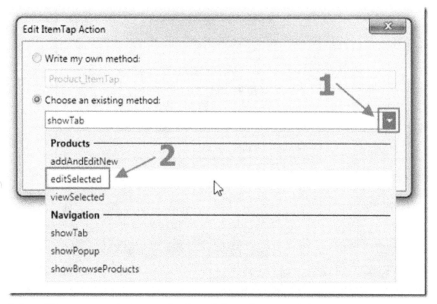

Select **Choose an existing method**, and then choose **editSelected**.

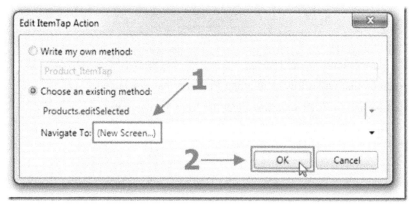

We will now connect the **Browse Data Screen** to a new **Edit Screen.**

For **Navigate To**, select **(New Screen…)** and click **OK**.

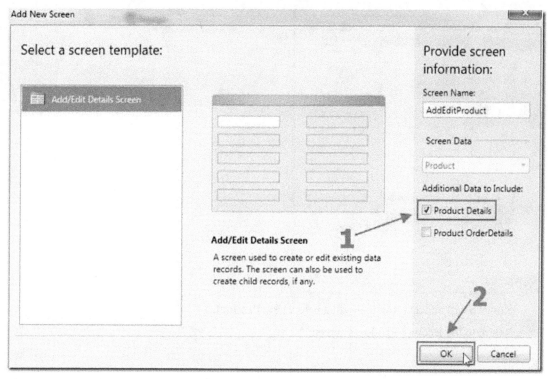

The **Add New Screen** box will show. Select only the **Product Details** and click **OK**.

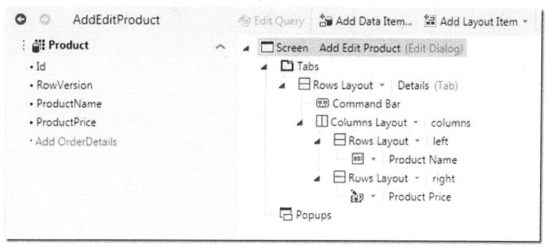

The screen will be created.

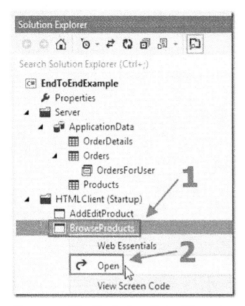

Now we will add a button that will create a new **Product**.

Return to the **Browse Products** screen.

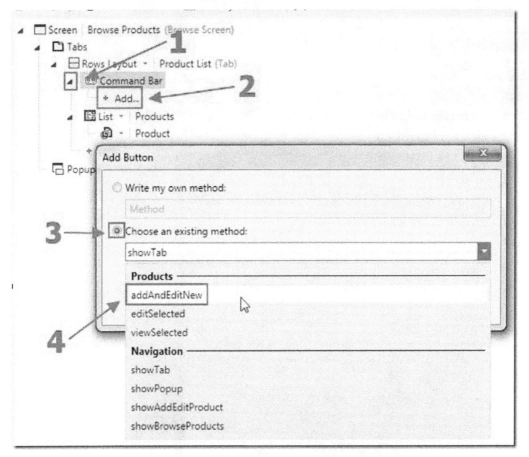

Select the **Command Bar**, then **Add**, then **Choose an existing method**, then **addAndEditNew**.

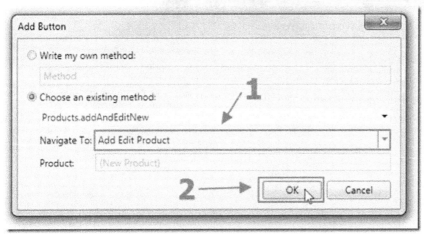

For **Navigate To**, select **Add Edit Product** (the screen created in the earlier step) and click **OK**.

Hit **F5** to run the application.

Click the **ADD PRODUCT** button to add a **Product**.

Add a product and click the **Save** button to save it.

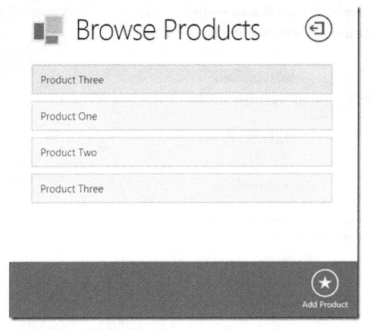

The products will show in a list.

Create the Main Page

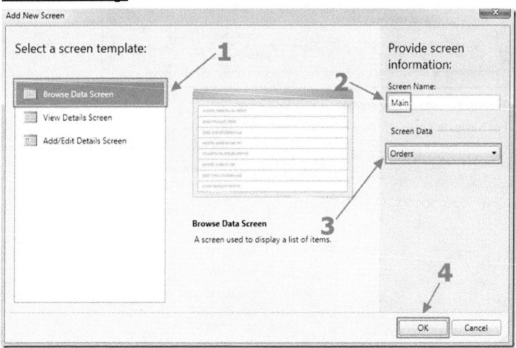

We will now create the **Main** screen. Return to **Visual Studio**.

Create a new screen called **Main** using the **Orders** table for **Screen Data**.

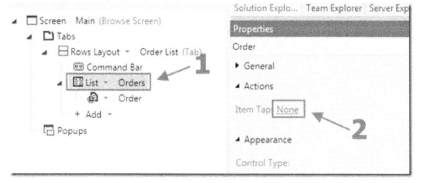

Select the **Item Tap** action for the **List** control.

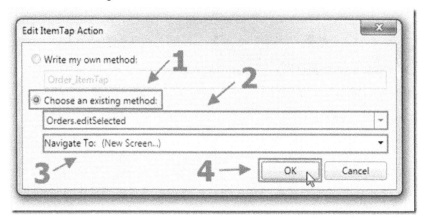

We will now connect the screen to a new **Edit** screen.

For **Navigate To**, select **(New Screen…)** and click **OK**.

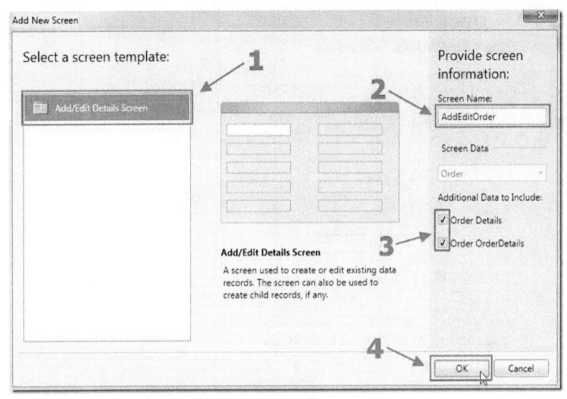

The **Add New Screen** box will show. Select **Order Details** and **Order OrderDetails** and click **OK**.

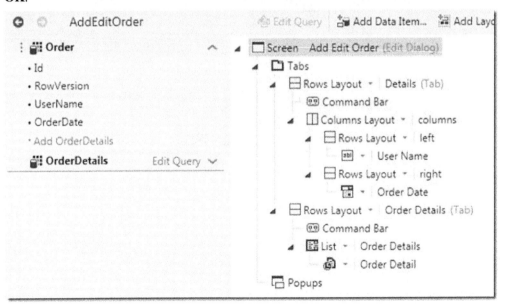

The screen will be created.

Format the Add Edit Order Screen

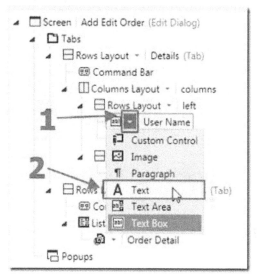

Change the **User Name Text Box** to a **Text** label.

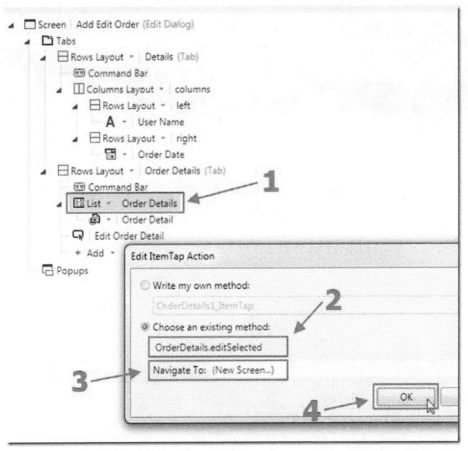

We will now allow the user to select an **Order Detail** and edit it in a new screen.

Click on the **Order Details** List control and then click on the **Tap** action in its **Properties**.

Select **OrderDetails.editSelected** and then **Navigate To: (New Screen…)**.

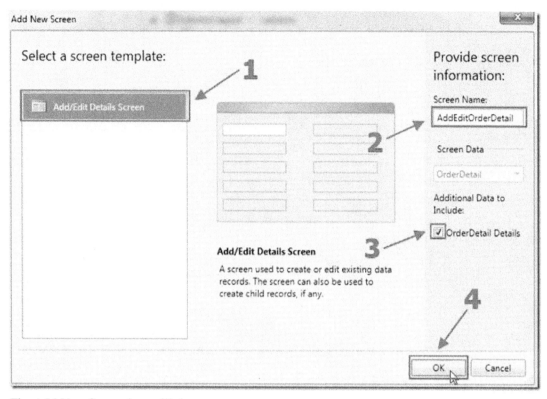

The **Add New Screen** box will show.

Select the **OrderDetail Details** and click **OK**.

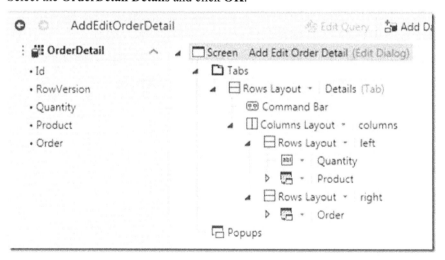

The screen will be created.

Format the Add Order Detail Edit Screen

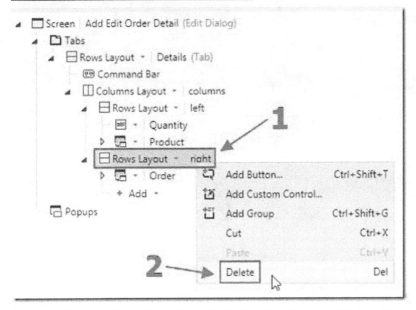

Right-click on the **Rows Layout** for the **Order** dropdown and **Delete** it.

We don't need to show the **Order** (and allow it to be changed) because it will be set by the time the user gets to this screen.

We will return to this screen later to add a **delete** button. That **delete** button will require custom **JavaScript** and we will show how to do that later.

Therefore, we are done with this screen for now.

Create an Add Order Detail Button

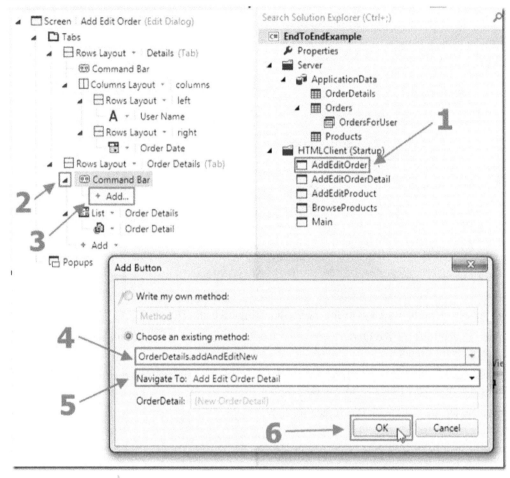

Now, we will create a button to allow the user to add a new **Order Detail**.

Return to the **AddEditOrder** screen.

Open the **Command Bar** for the **Order Details** Tab.

Select **Add** to add a new button.

In the **Add Button** popup, select **OrderDetails.addAndEditNew** and **Navigate To: Add Edit Order Detail** (the screen you created in the earlier step).

Create an Add Order Button

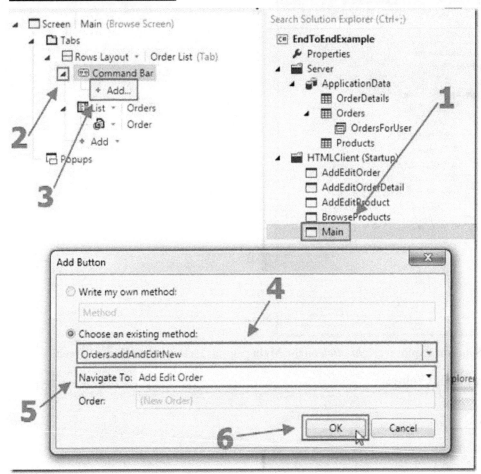

Next, we will create a button to allow the user to add a new **Order**.

Return to the **Main** screen.

Open the **Command Bar**.

Select **Add** to add a new button.

In the **Add Button** popup, select **Orders.addAndEditNew** and **Navigate To: Add Edit Order** (the screen you created in the earlier step).

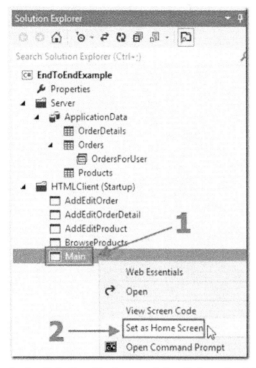

In the **Solution Explorer**, *right-click* on the **Main** page and select **Set as Home Screen**.

Setting Default Values

If we run the application and click the **Add Order** button…

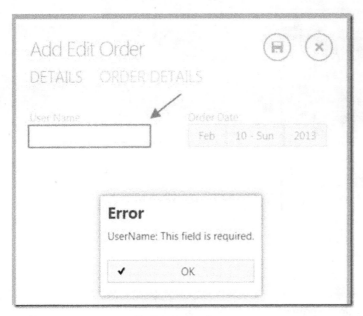

…then try to create an **Order**, it won't save.

We are missing the **User Name**. We have already added code to overwrite the **User Name** with the current user, but since we made it a required field, it must still be supplied. We could just make the **User Name** field a text box and allow the user to type it in, but we can use **ServerApplicationContext** to insert it client side automatically.

Using Server Application Context

We will now create a file handler that will use the Server Application Context API to retrieve the currently logged in user's **User Name**. We will then call that handler from **JavaScript** code on the client-side to fill in the value on the screen.

In the **Solution Explorer**, click on the project and switch to **File View**.

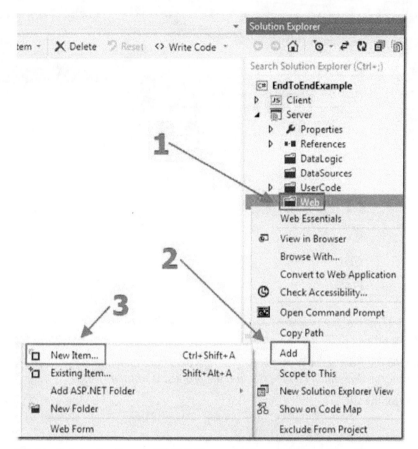

Right-click on the **Server/Web** folder and select **Add** then **New Item**.

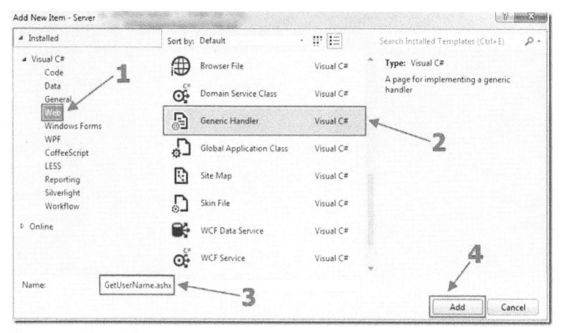

Create a new **Generic Handler**.

Note: You must create the file from scratch, so the proper references are added to the project. If you simply copy and paste, or drag and drop the file into the project, it will not work.

Use the following code for the file:

```
using System;
using System.Collections.Generic;
using System.Linq;
using System.Web;
namespace LightSwitchApplication.Web
{
    public class GetUserName : IHttpHandler
    {
        public void ProcessRequest(HttpContext context)
        {
            using (var serverContext = ServerApplicationContext.CreateContext())
            {
                context.Response.ContentType = "text/plain";
                context.Response.Write(serverContext.Application.User.Name);
            }
        }
        public bool IsReusable
        {
            get
            {
                return false;
            }
        }
    }
}
```

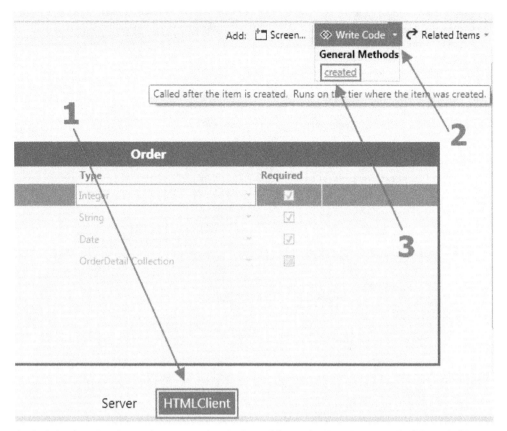

Switch back to **Logical View**, open the **Order** table, and select the **HTMLClient** (tab), **Write Code**, and then the *created* method.

Use the following code for the method:

```
myapp.Order.created = function (entity) {
    // Set the default date for the Order
    entity.OrderDate = new Date();
    // Using a Promise object we can call the CallGetUserName function
    msls.promiseOperation(CallGetUserName).then(function PromiseSuccess(PromiseResult) {
        // Set the result of the CallGetUserName function to the
        // UserName of the entity
        entity.UserName = PromiseResult;
    });
};

// This function will be wrapped in a Promise object
function CallGetUserName(operation) {
    $.ajax({
        type: 'post',
        data: {},
        url: '../web/GetUserName.ashx',
        success: operation.code(function AjaxSuccess(AjaxResult) {
            operation.complete(AjaxResult);
        })
    });
}
```

When we run the application, the **User Name** and **Date** are now set to their default values when a new record is created.

You will now be able to create and save records.

Formatting Output

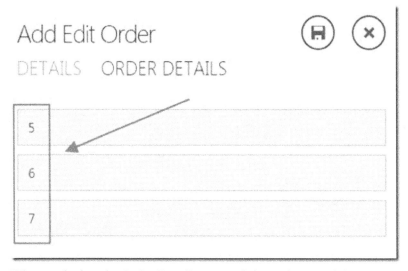

When we look at the **Order Details**, we see it is not formatted the way we want.

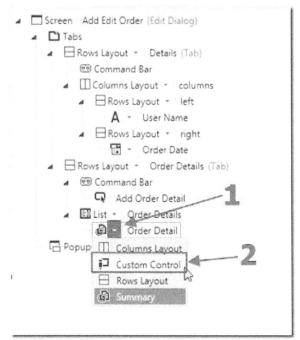

We return to the **Add Edit Order** screen and change the **Order Detail Summary** control to a **Custom Control**.

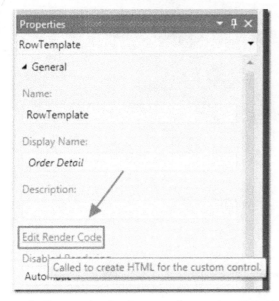

In the **Properties** for the control, we select **Edit Render Code**.

We use the following code:

```
myapp.AddEditOrder.RowTemplate_render = function (element, contentItem) {
    // We need to wait until the Products for the Order Detail are loaded
    // so we create a binding to "value.Product.ProductName"
    // When the data is loaded the binding will be raised
    // We will then have all the data required for our display
    contentItem.dataBind("value.Product.ProductName", function (newValue) {
        // clear the element
        element.innerHTML = "";
        // Create a template
        var itemTemplate = $("<div></div>");
        // Get the Product name and quantity
        var ProductName = contentItem.value.Product.ProductName;
        var ProductQuantity = "";
        if (contentItem.value.Quantity !== undefined) {
            ProductQuantity = ' [' + contentItem.value.Quantity + ']';
        }
        // Create the final display
        var FinalName = $("<h2>").text(ProductName + ProductQuantity);
        // Complete the template
        FinalName.appendTo($(itemTemplate));
        itemTemplate.appendTo($(element));
    });
};
```

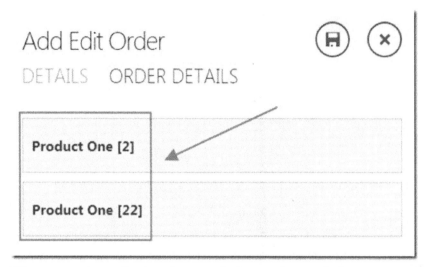

When we run the application, the output is formatted as we desire.

Calling a Custom Query

Next, we will call the query we created earlier.

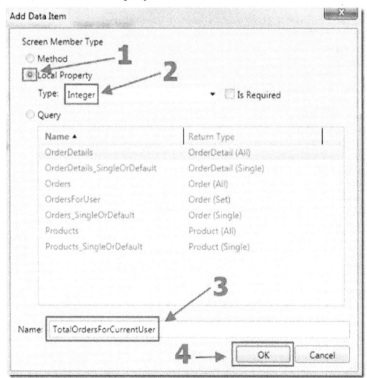

Open the **Main** screen, select **Add Data Item**, and create an **Integer** property.

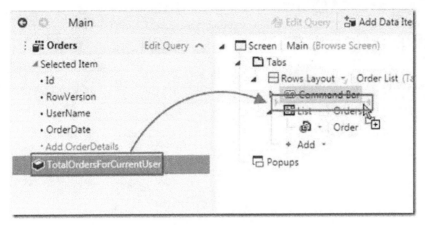

Drag and drop the property from the **View Model** to the screen layout.

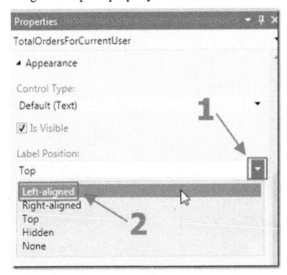

In the **Properties**, make the label **Left-aligned**.

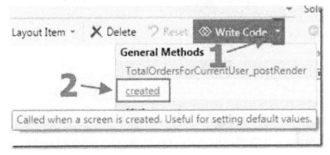

To set the value for the property, select **Write Code**, then the **created** method.

Use the following code:

```
myapp.Main.created = function (screen) {
    myapp.activeDataWorkspace.ApplicationData.OrdersForUser().execute().then(function (results) {
        var TotalCountOfOrders = CountOrders(results);
        screen.TotalOrdersForCurrentUser = TotalCountOfOrders.toString();
    });
};
function CountOrders(Orders) {
    var TotalOrders = 0;
    var orders = Orders.results;
    orders.forEach(function (order) {
        TotalOrders = TotalOrders + 1;
    });
    return TotalOrders;
}
```

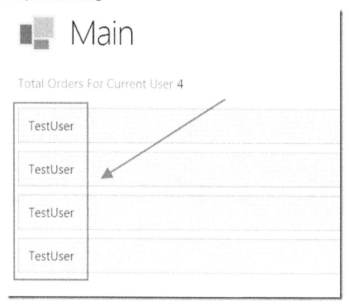

When we run the application we see a count of the **Orders**.

Easy Formatting

When we look at the **Main** screen, we see that it shows the **User Name**, and we would like to show the **Order Date**.

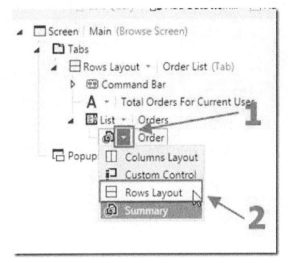

In **Visual Studio**, open the **Main** screen.

Change the **Order Summary** control to a **Rows Layout**.

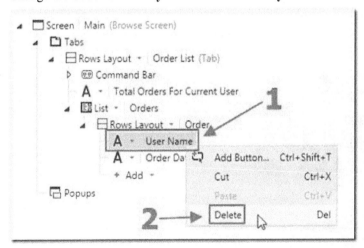

Right-click on the **User Name** label and delete it.

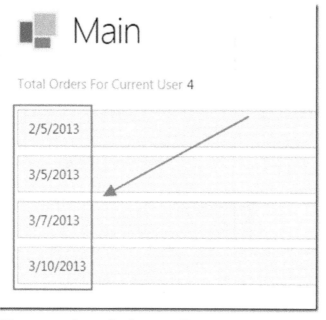

When we run the application, we will see the **Order Date**.

Deleting a Record

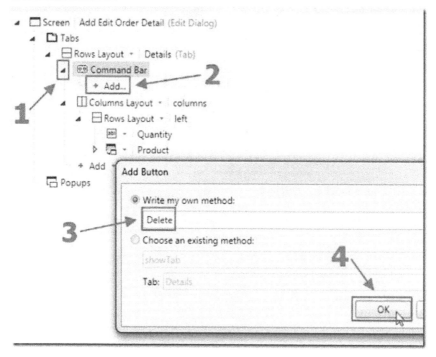

Open the **Add Edit Order Detail** screen and add a button to the **Command Bar**.

Make a **Delete** method for the button.

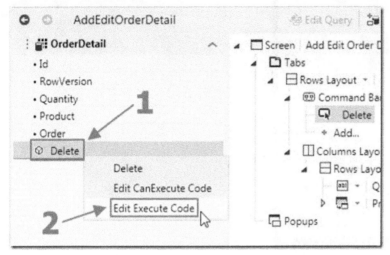

Right-click on the **Delete** method in the **View Model** and select **Edit Execute Code.**

Use the following code for the method:

```
myapp.AddEditOrderDetail.Delete_execute = function (screen) {
    screen.OrderDetail.deleteEntity();
    return myapp.commitChanges().then(null, function fail(e) {
        myapp.cancelChanges();
        throw e;
    });
};
```

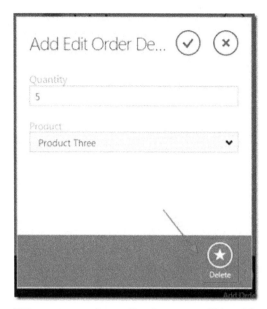

When you run the application, you will be able to delete the selected **Order Detail**.

You will need to **Save** the changes to actually delete the record.

We can also add a **Delete** button to the **Add Edit Order** screen using the following code:

```
myapp.AddEditOrder.Delete_execute = function (screen) {
    screen.Order.deleteEntity();
    myapp.commitChanges().then(null, function fail(e) {
        alert(e.message);
        myapp.cancelChanges();
        throw e;
    });
};
```

You will notice that if we try to delete an **Order** that still has **Order Detail** records...

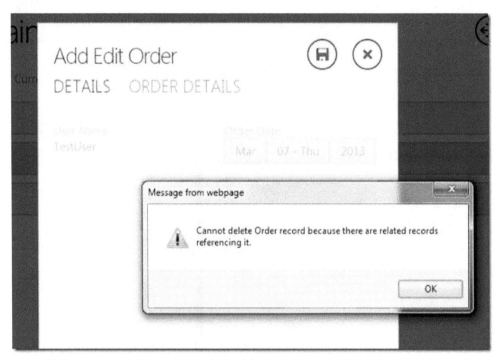

…it will throw an error because the relationship that we created between the tables earlier was set to not allow an **Order** to be deleted if there were associated records.

Delete all the **Order Details** first. Then you can delete the **Order**.

Navigate To a Screen

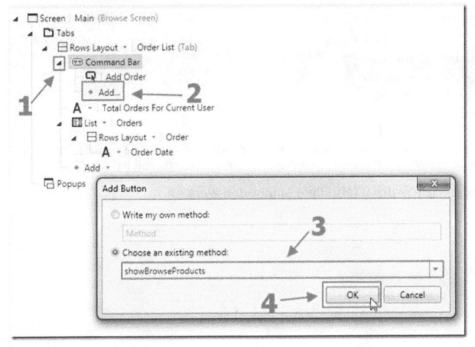

Open the **Main** screen and create a button that will navigate to the **Browse Products** screen.

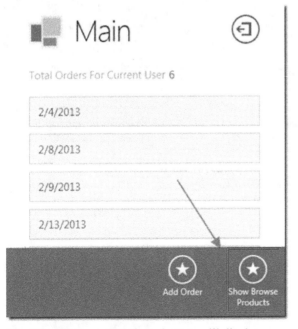

The **Show Browse Products** button will display.

Deploying Your LightSwitch application

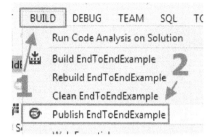

When your application is complete, select **Build** then **Publish** to access the wizard to deploy it. For more information see ***Deploying LightSwitch Applications*** (http://bit.ly/15k8JQr).

How Does A LightSwitch HTML Client Application Work?

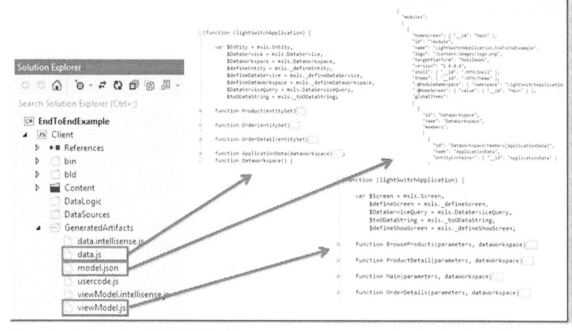

After using the **Visual Studio LightSwitch HTML Client**, you may wonder, how does it work? How does it turn the program we designed into an actual web application?

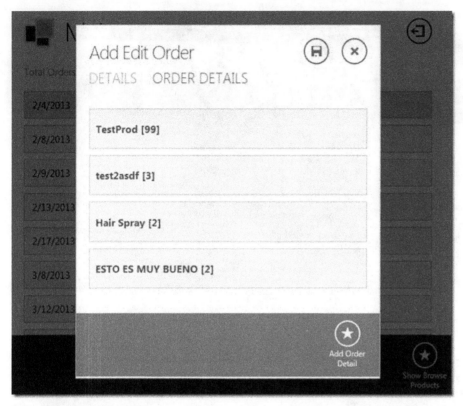

We will explore the application we just created.

The tool that will be most helpful will be **Fiddler**, available at http://fiddler2.com. This program will allow us to monitor the traffic that is transmitted between the web server running the **LightSwitch** application and our web browser.

#	Result	Protocol	Host	URL	Body	Caching
1	200	HTTP	Tunnel to	endtoendexample.lightswitchhelpwebsite.com:443	0	
2	200	HTTPS	endtoendexample.lightswitchhelpwebsite.com	/HTMLClient/	2,675	no-cache
3	200	HTTPS	endtoendexample.lightswitchhelpwebsite.com	/HTMLClient/Content/light-theme.css	23,965	no-cache
15	200	HTTPS	endtoendexample.lightswitchhelpwebsite.com	/HTMLClient/Content/msls-light.css	3,759	no-cache
16	200	HTTPS	endtoendexample.lightswitchhelpwebsite.com	/HTMLClient/Content/jquery.mobile.structure-1.2.0.min.css	47,307	no-cache
17	200	HTTPS	endtoendexample.lightswitchhelpwebsite.com	/HTMLClient/Scripts/winjs-1.0.min.js	14,883	no-cache
18	200	HTTPS	endtoendexample.lightswitchhelpwebsite.com	/HTMLClient/Scripts/msls-1.0.0.min.js	247,964	no-cache
19	200	HTTPS	endtoendexample.lightswitchhelpwebsite.com	/HTMLClient/Content/user-customization.css	1,467	no-cache
20	200	HTTPS	endtoendexample.lightswitchhelpwebsite.com	/HTMLClient/Scripts/Generated/generatedAssets.js	4,926	no-cache
21	200	HTTPS	endtoendexample.lightswitchhelpwebsite.com	/HTMLClient/Scripts/jquery.mobile-1.2.0.min.js	113,180	no-cache
22	200	HTTPS	endtoendexample.lightswitchhelpwebsite.com	/HTMLClient/Scripts/jquery-1.8.2.min.js	93,436	no-cache
23	200	HTTPS	endtoendexample.lightswitchhelpwebsite.com	/HTMLClient/Scripts/datajs-1.1.0.min.js	76,846	no-cache
24	200	HTTPS	endtoendexample.lightswitchhelpwebsite.com	/HTMLClient/Content/msls-1.0.0.min.css	40,629	no-cache
25	200	HTTPS	endtoendexample.lightswitchhelpwebsite.com	/HTMLClient/Scripts/Generated/resources.js	141	no-cache
26	200	HTTPS	endtoendexample.lightswitchhelpwebsite.com	/HTMLClient/Content/Images/msls-loader-light.gif	8,788	no-cache
27	200	HTTPS	endtoendexample.lightswitchhelpwebsite.com	/HTMLClient/Content/Images/user-splash-screen.png	1,538	no-cache
28	200	HTTPS	endtoendexample.lightswitchhelpwebsite.com	/HTMLClient/Content/Resources/msls.lang-EN-US.resjson	6,502	no-cache
29	404	HTTPS	endtoendexample.lightswitchhelpwebsite.com	/HTMLClient/Content/Resources/client.lang-EN-US.resjson	1,245	
30	404	HTTPS	endtoendexample.lightswitchhelpwebsite.com	/HTMLClient/Content/Resources/service.lang-EN-US.resjson	1,245	
31	200	HTTPS	endtoendexample.lightswitchhelpwebsite.com	/HTMLClient/Content/Resources/Generated/model.json	129,725	no-cache
32	200	HTTPS	endtoendexample.lightswitchhelpwebsite.com	/Microsoft.LightSwitch.SecurityData.svc/GetAuthenticationType	39	no-cache
33	200	HTTPS	endtoendexample.lightswitchhelpwebsite.com	/HTMLClient/Content/Images/user-logo.png	3,767	no-cache
34	200	HTTPS	endtoendexample.lightswitchhelpwebsite.com	/ApplicationData.svc/Orders?$top=45&$inlinecount=allpages	8,750	no-cache
35	200	HTTPS	endtoendexample.lightswitchhelpwebsite.com	/ApplicationData.svc/OrdersForUser()	8,731	no-cache
36	200	HTTPS	endtoendexample.lightswitchhelpwebsite.com	/HTMLClient/Content/images/ajax-loader.gif	7,825	no-cache
37	200	HTTPS	endtoendexample.lightswitchhelpwebsite.com	/HTMLClient/Content/images/msls-white-icons-36.png	11,570	no-cache
38	200	HTTPS	endtoendexample.lightswitchhelpwebsite.com	/HTMLClient/Content/images/msls-black-icons-36.png	12,587	no-cache
39	200	HTTPS	endtoendexample.lightswitchhelpwebsite.com	/HTMLClient/Content/Images/msls-loader-dark.gif	8,765	no-cache

When we run **Fiddler** and monitor the web traffic, we see that the application loads a number of files.

Note: The 404 errors in the image above are due to the sample application not employing any Localization.

All of these files are required to display the first page. We will also see as we use the application, it will transmit only a small amount of information—primarily the data required to display or update the application.

The HTML Page

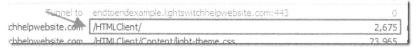

Everything starts with the **HTML** page.

```
        <link rel="stylesheet" type="text/css" href="Content/light-theme.css" />
        <link rel="stylesheet" type="text/css" href="Content/msls-light.css" />

        <link rel="stylesheet" type="text/css" href="Content/jquery.mobile.structure-1.2.0.min.css" />
        <link rel="stylesheet" type="text/css" href="Content/msls-1.0.0.min.css" />

        <!-- Default font, header, and icon styles can be overriden in user-customization.css -->
        <link rel="stylesheet" type="text/css" href="Content/user-customization.css"/>
</head>
<body>
        <div id="msls-id-app-loading" class="ui-body-a msls-layout-ignore">
            <div class="msls-app-loading-img"></div>
            <span class="ui-icon ui-icon-loading"></span>
            <div class="ui-bottom-load">
                <div>EndToEndExample</div>
            </div>
        </div>

        <script type="text/javascript" src="//ajax.aspnetcdn.com/ajax/globalize/0.1.1/globalize.min.js"></script>
        <script type="text/javascript" src="Scripts/winjs-1.0.min.js"></script>
        <script type="text/javascript" src="Scripts/jquery-1.8.2.min.js"></script>
        <script type="text/javascript" src="Scripts/jquery.mobile-1.2.0.min.js"></script>
        <script type="text/javascript" src="Scripts/datajs-1.1.0.min.js"></script>
        <script type="text/javascript" src="Scripts/Generated/resources.js"></script>
        <script type="text/javascript" src="Scripts/msls-1.0.0.min.js"></script>
        <script type="text/javascript" src="Scripts/Generated/generatedAssets.js"></script>
        <script type="text/javascript">
```

When we look at the contents of the page, we see it loads the **.css** files and **.js** scripts that the **LightSwitch** application requires.

The **JavaScript** library files that it loads are:

- **jquery/ jquery.mobile**
  - JavaScript libraries that provide cross browser functionality

- **msls**
  - The primary LightSwitch framework library that provides the application functionality

- **winjs**
  - A helper library for things such as Promise objects that handle asynchronous calls

- **datajs**
  - Used to provide OData communication

msls.js and winjs.js

te.com	/HTMLClient/Content/jquery.mobile.structure-1.2.0.min.css	47,307	nc
te.com	/HTMLClient/Scripts/winjs-1.0.min.js	14,883	nc
te.com	/HTMLClient/Scripts/msls-1.0.0.min.js	247,964	nc
te.com	/HTMLClient/Content/user-customization.css	1,467	nc

The **msls.js** library is the heart of the **LightSwitch** framework. There is an enormous amount of functionality in this file. Much of it you can reference in your custom code.

```
);
msls_initDataService =
function initDataService(dataService, dataWorkspace) {
    if (dataWorkspace) {
        dataService.details.dataWorkspace = dataWorkspace;
    }
};

function getChanges() {
    /// <summary>
    /// Gets the entities tracked by this data service that
    /// have been added, modified or marked for deletion.
    /// </summary>
    /// <returns type="Array" elementType="msls.Entity">
    /// The entities that have been added, modified or marked for deletion.
    /// </returns>
    var changes = [];
    $.each(this.properties.all(), function () {
        var entitySet = this.value;
        changes = changes.concat(entitySet._addedEntities);
        $.each(entitySet._loadedEntities, function () {
            if (this.details.entityState !== _EntityState.unchanged) {
```

Search Solution Explorer (Ctrl+;)

- Screens
- ▲ Scripts
  - datajs-1.1.0.js
  - datajs-1.1.0.min.js
  - jquery.mobile-1.2.0.js
  - jquery.mobile-1.2.0.min.js
  - jquery.mobile-1.2.0-vsdoc.js
  - jquery-1.8.2.intellisense.js
  - jquery-1.8.2.js
  - jquery-1.8.2.min.js
  - msls-1.0.0.js
  - msls-1.0.0.min.js
  - msls-1.0.0-vsdoc.js
  - winjs-1.0.js
  - winjs-1.0.min.js
- ▷ UserCode
- default.htm
- ModelManifest.xml
- packages.config

The best way to explore it is to open the **msls-vsdoc.js** file in the **Scripts** directory and read the comments.

GetAuthenticationType

During the application start-up process, the **msls.js** library makes a call to the **SecurityData.svc** service to determine what the authentication type for the application is. If **Forms Authentication** is detected, the **LightSwitch** client will display the *logout* button.

generatedAssets.js / usercode.js

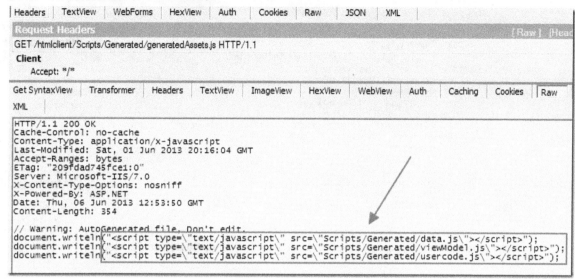

The **generatedAssets.js** file is referenced in the **default.htm** page.

It contains code that loads other required **JavaScript** libraries and files.

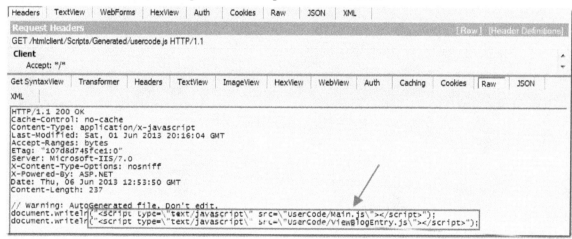

The **usercode.js** file (loaded in the **generatedAssets.js** file) loads the **JavaScript** files that contain custom code that we have created.

model.json

/HTMLClient/Content/Resources/Generated/model.json   129,725

The structure of the application is contained in the **model.json** file.

```
2   {
3     "modules":
4     [
5       {
6         "homeScreen": { "__id": "Main" },
7         "id": "!module",
8         "name": "LightSwitchApplication.EndToEndExample",
9         "logo": "/Content/Images/logo.png",
10        "targetPlatform": "MobileWeb",
11        "version": "1.0.0.0",
12        "shell": { "__id": ":HTMLShell" },
13        "theme": { "__id": ":HTMLTheme" },
14        ":@ModuleNamespace": { "namespace": "LightSwitchApplication" },
15        ":@HomeScreen": { "value": { "__id": "Main" } },
16        "globalItems":
17        [
18          {
19            "id": "DataWorkspace",
20            "name": "DataWorkspace",
21            "members":
22            [
```

The **model.json** file is created each time we build the **LightSwitch** application.

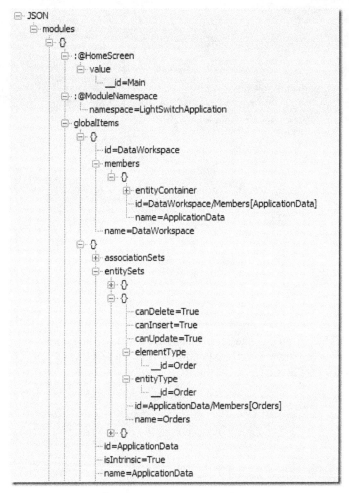

```
JSON
  modules
    {}
      : @HomeScreen
        value
          __id=Main
      : @ModuleNamespace
        namespace=LightSwitchApplication
      globalItems
        {}
          id=DataWorkspace
          members
            {}
              entityContainer
              id=DataWorkspace/Members[ApplicationData]
              name=ApplicationData
          name=DataWorkspace
        {}
          associationSets
          entitySets
            {}
            {}
              canDelete=True
              canInsert=True
              canUpdate=True
              elementType
                __id=Order
              entityType
                __id=Order
              id=ApplicationData/Members[Orders]
              name=Orders
            {}
          id=ApplicationData
          isIntrinsic=True
          name=ApplicationData
```

The file is in **JSON** format and describes the entire application. When this is loaded, the application has all the information it needs to run, except for the data.

The Screen

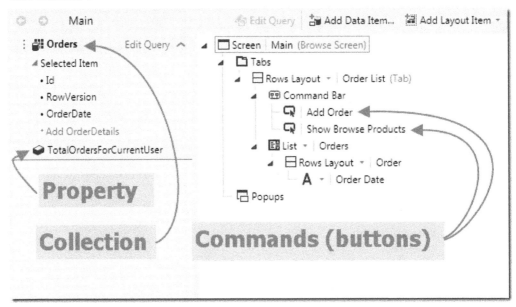

When we look at a screen in the **LightSwitch** designer, we see that it consists of **Properties**, **Collections** and **Commands**. This is consistent with the **MVVM** (Model-View-View Model) structure of the **LightSwitch Silverlight Client**.

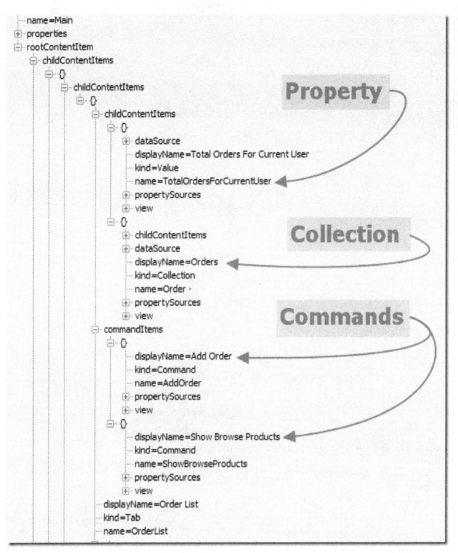

```
name=Main
properties
rootContentItem
    childContentItems
        ◊
            childContentItems
                ◊
                    childContentItems
                        ◊
                            dataSource
                            displayName=Total Orders For Current User
                            kind=Value
                            name=TotalOrdersForCurrentUser          Property
                            propertySources
                            view
                        ◊
                            childContentItems
                            dataSource
                            displayName=Orders                       Collection
                            kind=Collection
                            name=Order
                            propertySources
                            view
                    commandItems                                     Commands
                        ◊
                            displayName=Add Order
                            kind=Command
                            name=AddOrder
                            propertySources
                            view
                        ◊
                            displayName=Show Browse Products
                            kind=Command
                            name=ShowBrowseProducts
                            propertySources
                            view
                    displayName=Order List
                    kind=Tab
                    name=OrderList
```

When we look at the same screen in the **model.json** file, we see it defines the structure of the screens.

```
function Main(parameters, dataWorkspace) {
    /// <summary>
    /// Represents the Main screen.
    /// </summary>
    /// <param name="parameters" type="Array">
    /// An array of screen parameter values.
    /// </param>
    /// <param name="dataWorkspace" type="msls.application.DataWorkspace" optional="true">
    /// An existing data workspace for this screen to use. By default, a new data workspace is created.
    /// </param>
    /// <field name="Orders" type="msls.VisualCollection" elementType="msls.application.Order">
    /// Gets the orders for this screen.
    /// </field>
    /// <field name="TotalOrdersForCurrentUser" type="Number">
    /// Gets or sets the totalOrdersForCurrentUser for this screen.
    /// </field>
    /// <field name="details" type="msls.application.Main.Details">
    /// Gets the details for this screen.
    /// </field>
    if (!dataWorkspace) {
        dataWorkspace = new lightSwitchApplication.DataWorkspace();
    }
    $Screen.call(this, dataWorkspace, "Main", parameters);
}
msls._addToNamespace("msls.application", {

    Main: $defineScreen(Main, [
        {
            name: "Orders", kind: "collection", elementType: lightSwitchApplication.Order,
            createQuery: function () {
                return this.dataWorkspace.ApplicationData.Orders;
            }
        },
        { name: "TotalOrdersForCurrentUser", kind: "local", type: Number }
    ], [
    ]),
    showMain: $defineShowScreen(function showMain(options) {
        /// <summary>
        /// Asynchronously navigates forward to the Main screen.
        /// </summary>
        /// <param name="options" optional="true">
        /// An object that provides one or more of the following options:<br/>- beforeShown:
        /// a function that is called after boundary behavior has been applied but before the screen is shown.
        /// <br/>+ Signature: beforeShown(screen)<br/>- afterClosed: a function that is called after boundary
        /// behavior has been applied and the screen has been closed.<br/>+ Signature:
        /// afterClosed(screen, action : msls.NavigateBackAction)
        /// </param>
        /// <returns type="WinJS.Promise" />
        var parameters = Array.prototype.slice.call(arguments, 0, 0);
        return lightSwitchApplication.showScreen("Main", parameters, options);
    }),
```

The **viewModel.js** library defines the **JavaScript** representation of the screens and allows programmatic access to the screens.

The Data

```
ApplicationData: $defineDataService(ApplicationData, lightSwitchApplication.rootUri + "/ApplicationData.svc", [
    { name: "Products", elementType: Product },
    { name: "Orders", elementType: Order },
    { name: "OrderDetails", elementType: OrderDetail }
], [
    {
        name: "Products_SingleOrDefault", value: function (Id) {
            return new $DataServiceQuery({ _entitySet: this.Products },
                lightSwitchApplication.rootUri + "/ApplicationData.svc" +
                "/Products(" + "Id=" + $toODataString(Id, "Int32?") + ")"
            );
        }
    },
    {
        name: "Orders_SingleOrDefault", value: function (Id) {
            return new $DataServiceQuery({ _entitySet: this.Orders },
                lightSwitchApplication.rootUri + "/ApplicationData.svc"
                + "/Orders(" + "Id=" + $toODataString(Id, "Int32?") + ")"
            );
        }
    },
    {
        name: "OrderDetails_SingleOrDefault", value: function (Id) {
            return new $DataServiceQuery({ _entitySet: this.OrderDetails },
                lightSwitchApplication.rootUri + "/ApplicationData.svc"
                + "/OrderDetails(" + "Id=" + $toODataString(Id, "Int32?") + ")"
            );
        }
    }
]),
```

The **data.js** library contains a representation of all the data assets in the **LightSwitch** application.

It also contains the location of the **.svc** services that are used to actually retrieve the data from the server.

```
5618    msls_mixIntoExistingClass(_DataServiceQuery, {
5619        execute: function execute() {
5620            var me = this,
5621                current = me,
5622                afterQueryExecuted;
5623            do [...]
5630
5631            if (afterQueryExecuted) [...]
5652        },
5653        _requestUri: msls_accessorProperty(
5654            function _requestUri_get() {
5655                var requestUri,
5656                    current = this, i,
5657                    filters = [],
5658                    skip,
5659                    take,
5660                    includeTotalCount,
5661                    orderBys = [],
5662                    expands = [],
5663                    options = [];
5664                do [...]
5699                if (current._queryParameters) [...]
5706                if (filters.length > 0) [...]
5709                if (orderBys.length > 0) [...]
5712                if (expands.length > 0) [...]
5715                if (typeof skip === "number") [...]
5718                if (typeof take === "number") [...]
5721                if (includeTotalCount) [...]
5724                if (options.length > 0) [...]
5727                return requestUri;
5728                        requestUri  Q ▾ "http://localhost:6448/ApplicationData.svc/Orders?$top=45&$inlinecount=allpages"
5729            )
5730    });
```

At this point, the **msls.js** library has access to all the information required to obtain the data needed by the application.

In this example, it knows from the **model.json** library that the first page contains the orders collection. It constructs a query using properties from the **data.js** library to retrieve the data.

Updating Data

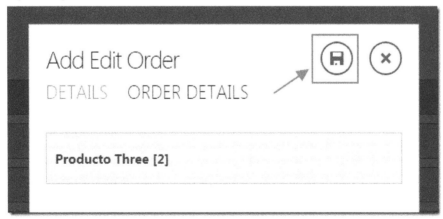

The application is now very efficient; it only needs to contact the server to retrieve data and images.

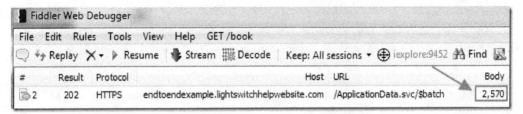

When we click the **Save** button while adding a single order detail, it causes only one small request to the webserver.

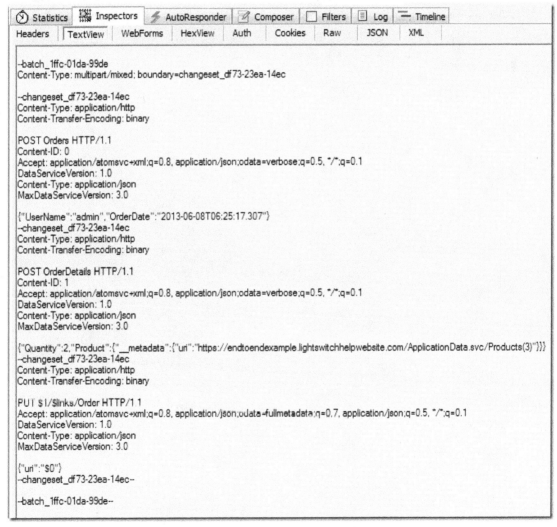

--batch_1ffc-01da-99de
Content-Type: multipart/mixed; boundary=changeset_df73-23ea-14ec

--changeset_df73-23ea-14ec
Content-Type: application/http
Content-Transfer-Encoding: binary

POST Orders HTTP/1.1
Content-ID: 0
Accept: application/atomsvc+xml;q=0.8, application/json;odata=verbose;q=0.5, */*;q=0.1
DataServiceVersion: 1.0
Content-Type: application/json
MaxDataServiceVersion: 3.0

{"UserName":"admin","OrderDate":"2013-06-08T06:25:17.307"}
--changeset_df73-23ea-14ec
Content-Type: application/http
Content-Transfer-Encoding: binary

POST OrderDetails HTTP/1.1
Content-ID: 1
Accept: application/atomsvc+xml;q=0.8, application/json;odata=verbose;q=0.5, */*;q=0.1
DataServiceVersion: 1.0
Content-Type: application/json
MaxDataServiceVersion: 3.0

{"Quantity":2,"Product":{"__metadata":{"uri":"https://endtoendexample.lightswitchhelpwebsite.com/ApplicationData.svc/Products(3)"}}}
--changeset_df73-23ea-14ec
Content-Type: application/http
Content-Transfer-Encoding: binary

PUT $1/$links/Order HTTP/1.1
Accept: application/atomsvc+xml;q=0.8, application/json;odata=fullmetadata;q=0.7, application/json;q=0.5, */*;q=0.1
DataServiceVersion: 1.0
Content-Type: application/json
MaxDataServiceVersion: 3.0

{"uri":"$0"}
--changeset_df73-23ea-14ec--

--batch_1ffc-01da-99de--

Inserting or updating in the application requires only a small data payload.

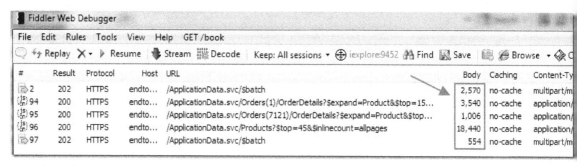

After inserting and updating several records, we see only the data service calls are needed.

Chapter 3: The LightSwitch HTML Client API

The sample code for this chapter can be obtained at the links "Writing JavaScript That Implements The Binding Pattern In Visual Studio LightSwitch" and " Using Promises In Visual Studio LightSwitch" at http://lightswitchhelpwebsite.com/Downloads.aspx

Now that we have seen some of the capabilities of the **LightSwitch HTML Client**, we are ready to learn how to use this incredibly productive tool. We will explore the most important parts of the Application Programming Interface (the API).

The Binding Pattern

The **binding pattern** has several advantages in that it allows you to create large robust and well-structured applications. You may have heard about the binding pattern in **Silverlight** and **WPF** (known as Model-View-View Model or MVVM). The key component is the **NotifyPropertyChanged** interface that raises an event when anything changes a property that implements the interface.

```
public string CustomerName
{
    get
    {
        return this.customerNameValue;
    }

    set
    {
        if (value != this.customerNameValue)
        {
            this.customerNameValue = value;
            NotifyPropertyChanged();
        }
    }
}
```

The ability to bind to a property (this can be a single scalar value or an entity composed of several properties) allows you to simply subscribe to changes in say the *First Name* property, and in one place, validate, update, or persist the value in one or more centralized methods. Without binding, you would need to implement *if...then* code in a multitude of places, potentially creating *spaghetti code* (the larger your application gets).

Incorporate Toastr into LightSwitch

To visually show data binding in **LightSwitch**, we will use the **Toastr JavaScript** plug-in. To install the **Toastr** plug-in, we create a **LightSwitch** project and switch to **File View**.

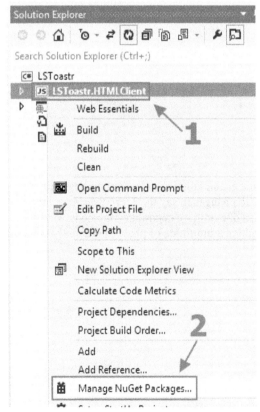

Next, we *right-click* on the **Client** project, and select **Manage NuGet Packages**.

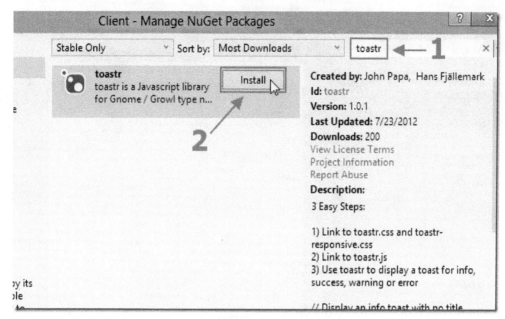

We search for the **Toastr** project, and click the **Install** button.

This will automatically download and install the required files in the project.

```
    <!-- Change light-theme.css and msls-light.css to dark-theme.css and msls-dark.css respectively to use the
         dark theme.  Alternatively, you may replace light-theme.css with a custom jQuery Mobile theme. -->
    <link rel="stylesheet" type="text/css" href="Content/light-theme.css" />
    <link rel="stylesheet" type="text/css" href="Content/msls-light.css" />

    <link rel="stylesheet" type="text/css" href="Content/jquery.mobile.structure-1.2.0.min.css" />
    <link rel="stylesheet" type="text/css" href="Content/msls-1.0.0.min.css" />
    <link rel="stylesheet" type="text/css" href="Content/toastr.css" />

    <!-- Default font, header, and icon styles can be overriden in user-customization.css -->
    <link rel="stylesheet" type="text/css" href="Content/user-customization.css"/>
</head>
<body>
    <div id="msls-id-app-loading" class="ui-body-a msls-layout-ignore">
        <div class="msls-app-loading-img"></div>
        <span class="ui-icon ui-icon-loading"></span>
        <div class="ui-bottom-load">
            <div>LSToastr</div>
        </div>
    </div>

    <script type="text/javascript" src="//ajax.aspnetcdn.com/ajax/globalize/0.1.1/globalize.min.js"></script>
    <script type="text/javascript" src="Scripts/winjs-1.0.min.js"></script>
    <script type="text/javascript" src="Scripts/jquery-1.8.2.min.js"></script>
    <script type="text/javascript" src="Scripts/jquery.mobile-1.2.0.min.js"></script>
    <script type="text/javascript" src="Scripts/datajs-1.1.0.min.js"></script>
    <script type="text/javascript" src="Scripts/Generated/resources.js"></script>
    <script type="text/javascript" src="Scripts/msls-1.0.0.min.js"></script>
    <script type="text/javascript" src="Scripts/Generated/generatedAssets.js"></script>
    <script type="text/javascript" src="Scripts/toastr.js"></script>
    <script type="text/javascript">
        $(document).ready(function () {
            msls._run()
            .then(null, function failure(error) {
                alert(error);
            });
        });
    </script>
```

Next, we open the **default.htm** page, and add references to the **toastr.css** file and the **toastr.js** file.

Binding In the LightSwitch HTML Client

Two methods to bind to data will be explored, **dataBind** and **addChangeListener**. **dataBind** is a function that actually implements **addChangeListener**. **dataBind** provides the advantage in that it parses the input binding path that you specify and creates change notifications (using **addChangeListener**).

Each change notification will raise the callback function that you specify in the **dataBind** constructor. On the other hand, **addChangeListener** will just bind to the element that you specify. **addChangeListener** has the advantage; unlike **dataBind**, it does not require a **contentItem,** so it can be used in entity code that does not have a **contentItem**.

dataBind

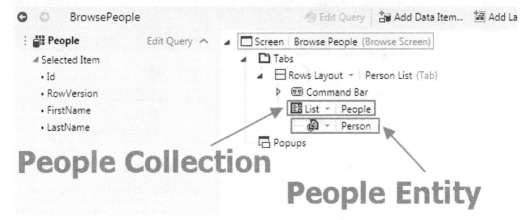

A great feature about **LightSwitch** is that it allows you to easily see what you are binding to.

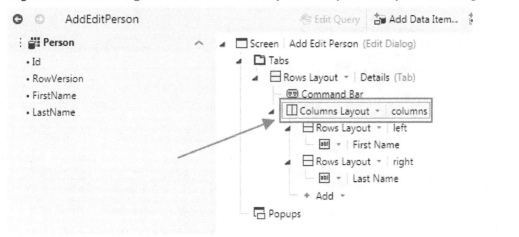

To bind to data, you click on the element you want to bind to in the screen designer.

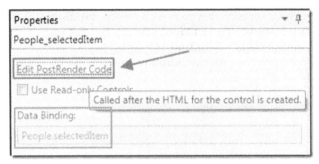

In the **Properties** for the element, you can click **Edit PostRender Code**.

This will take you to a **JavaScript** method that is **wired-up** and ready for your custom code.

We will start off by displaying the initial values, using the **Toastr** plug-in, by adding the following code to the method:

```
myapp.AddEditPerson.columns_postRender = function (element, contentItem) {

    // Display Initial Values
    var FirstName = contentItem.value.FirstName;
    var LastName = contentItem.value.LastName;

    var InitialValues = 'Initial Values:'
                    + ' FirstName = '
                    + FirstName
                    + ' LastName = '
                    + LastName;

    toastr.info(InitialValues);
```

When we run the application, the initial values are displayed.

However, when we change the values, in order to see the new values, we have to save the record and re-open it.

To resolve this and provide the *NotifyPropertyChanged like* binding notifications, we use the following code:

```
myapp.AddEditPerson.columns_postRender = function (element, contentItem) {

    // Binding to only the FirstName property
    contentItem.dataBind("value.FirstName", function (newValue) {

        var newFirstName = newValue;

        var updatedFirstNameOnly = 'Updated FirstNameOnly: '
                                   + newFirstName;

        toastr.info(updatedFirstNameOnly);
    });

};
```

Also, note that the *initial scope* is the entire **People** entity, which consists of **FirstName** and **LastName**, but in this case we are only binding to the **FirstName** property because we set **dataBind** binding to **"value.FirstName"**.

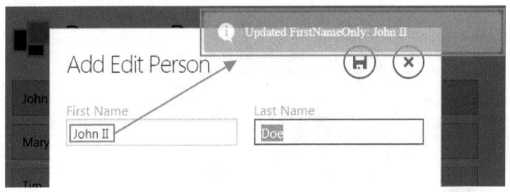

When we run the application, the **Toastr** notification will show the latest value each time we change it (and tab out of the box).

The following code shows how to bind to the property that indicates if a property is "dirty" (has been changed):

```
    // Binding to LastName isChanged property
    contentItem.dataBind("value.details.properties.LastName.isChanged", function (newValue) {

        var isChangedLastName = 'LastName.isChanged: '
                                + newValue;

        toastr.info(isChangedLastName);
    });
```

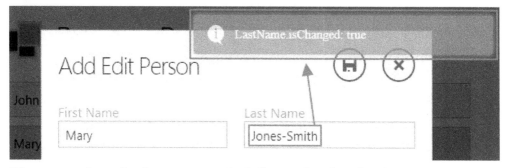

When we run the application, we can see the indicator when the value changes.

When and Where to use it

Use it within a **render** or **postRender** function. This allows you to easily get notified when some property (that is reachable from the **contentItem**) has changed, regardless of how deeply nested the data is.

Limitations

dataBind requires a **contentItem** and you don't have that in a **Screen** or **Entity** method; however, in a **Screen** method, you can use code such as: *contentItem = screen.findContentItem("OrderDate") to get a specific content item.*

addChangeListener

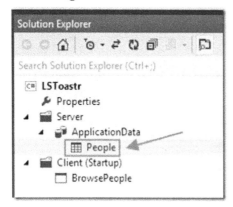

We can open a table (entity).

We select the **HTMLClient** tab, then the **Write Code** menu. We then select the **created** method.

```
1   /// <reference path="../GeneratedArtifacts/viewModel.js" />
2
3 ⊟myapp.Person.created = function (entity) {
4       // Write code here.
5   |
6   };
```

Unlike the *render* methods, we only have access to **entity**; therefore, we must use
addChangeListener.

Add the following code:

```
entity.addChangeListener("LastName", function (e) {
    toastr.info("(from entity level) LastName value changed to: " + entity.LastName);
});
```

 Browse People

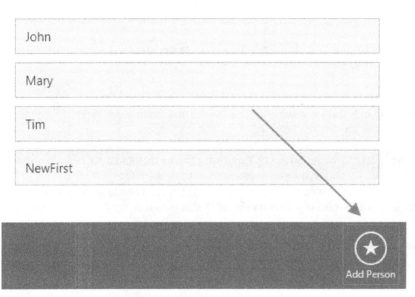

| John |
| Mary |
| Tim |
| NewFirst |

Add Person

When we run the application, we have to create a new entity to invoke the **addChangeListener**.

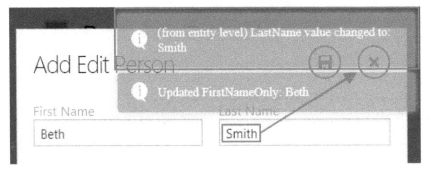

The notification will fire without the need to save the record first.

When and Where to use it

Use it from within **Entity** and **Screen** functions. This code will work anywhere you show the data, avoiding the need to duplicate the logic on each screen the data object appears on.

Limitations

It does not have the ability to specify a binding path to listen to nested data.

Promises

To create responsive HTML applications (using **JavaScript**), you will need to use *asynchronous* calls to communicate with external resources. While you can make requests *synchronously*, it is a bad practice because it locks up the web browser.

Asynchronous code isn't easy to write; however, there are patterns that make it easier. In .NET there are classes like **Task<T>** that allow you to *await* on asynchronous code. This code is easier to write because it looks like synchronous code. To write asynchronous code in **JavaScript**, we have the **Promise** object. A **Promise** object is *an object that acts as a proxy for a result that is initially unknown.*

In order to communicate with remote resources from code, you need to write asynchronous code.

Promise objects are one possible way of managing asynchronous work that **LightSwitch** has adopted.

WinJS Promise objects represent the specific implementation of **Promises** that the **LightSwitch** runtime understands.

Promise Objects in LightSwitch

In **LightSwitch**, **Promise** objects are produced by calling *async* methods. For example, the **OrdersForUser** query in the image above is an *async* method, and it returns a **Promise** object.

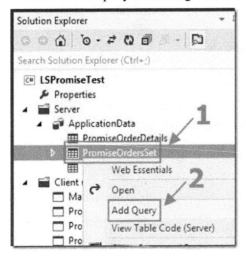

We can create a server side query by selecting **Add Query** after *right-clicking* on a table.

We then use the following code:

```
partial void OrdersForUser_PreprocessQuery(ref IQueryable<PromiseOrders> query)
{
    // Only show the Orders for the current user
    query = query.Where(x => x.UserName == this.Application.User.Identity.Name);
}
```

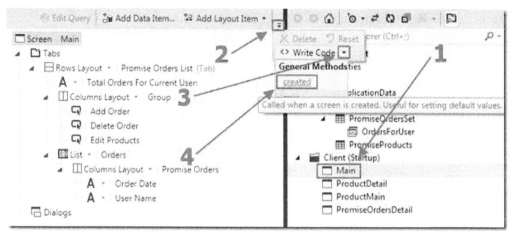

We open the **Screen** and select the **Created** method.

```
pp.Main.created = function (screen) {
  myapp.activeDataWorkspace.ApplicationData.OrdersForUser().execute().then(function (results) {
    var TotalCountOfOrders = CountOrders(results);
    screen.TotalOrdersForCurrentUser = TotalCountOfO
});
```

WinJS.Promise execute()
Asynchronously executes this query and returns a promise that is fulfilled when the query has been executed.

If we try to directly call the query, we find it does not return the expected value. Instead, it returns a **Promise** object.

To consume the **Promise** object, we use the following code:

```
myapp.Main.created = function (screen) {
    myapp.activeDataWorkspace.ApplicationData.OrdersForUser()
        .execute().then(function (results) {
        var TotalCountOfOrders = CountOrders(results);
        screen.TotalOrdersForCurrentUser = TotalCountOfOrders.toString();
    });
};

function CountOrders(Orders) {
    var TotalOrders = 0;
    var orders = Orders.results;
    orders.forEach(function (order) {
        TotalOrders = TotalOrders + 1;
    });
    return TotalOrders;
}
```

When we run the application, we see that the code works as expected.

The Then Method

```
ationData.OrdersForUser().execute().then(function (results) {
    = CountOrders(results);
```

A **Promise** object has one interesting method, the ***then*** method.

Note: It is not recommended that you use the done method because the scenarios for its proper use are few.

With the ***then*** method, you can specify code that is called when the asynchronous work has completed—either with an error or successfully.

Calling the msls.promiseOperation directly

We can use the **msls.promiseOperation** method to wrap any asynchronous call that we need to make. **Tip:** To maintain the most predictable coding experience, the best way to create your own **Promise** objects is to use the **msls.promiseOperation()** method.

Let's look at an example that demonstrates how we can use this method to encapsulate *async* methods.

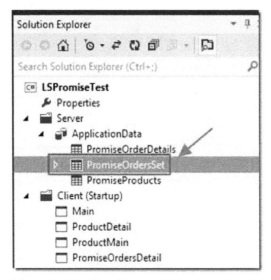

First, we open the table.

Next, we click the **HTMLClient** tab.

This switches us to the client side code that will interact with the entity; this code will be written in **JavaScript** and run on the client.

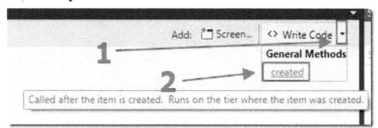

We then select the **Created** method.

We use the following code for the method:

```
myapp.PromiseOrders.created = function (entity) {
    // Set the default date for the Order
    entity.OrderDate = new Date();
    // Using a Promise object we can call the CallGetUserName function
    msls.promiseOperation(CallGetUserName)
        .then(function PromiseSuccess(PromiseResult) {
            // Set the result of the CallGetUserName function to the
            // UserName of the entity
            entity.UserName = PromiseResult;
        });
};


// This function will be wrapped in a Promise object
function CallGetUserName(operation) {
    $.ajax({
        type: 'post',
        data: {},
        url: '../web/GetUserName.ashx',
        success: operation.code(function AjaxSuccess(AjaxResult) {
            operation.complete(AjaxResult);
        })
    });
}
```

A few things to note about the code above:

The **CallGetUserName** method is passed an *operation* that is being set to *complete* in the success parameter of the **JQuery Ajax** call. If we do not do this, the **Promise** operation will not know when it is complete.

The *complete* method lets us pass an optional value to the calling method; in this case we are passing the *user name* retrieved.

The advantage of using the **msls.promiseOperation** in this example is it allows us to wrap the **JQuery Ajax** call. This enables us to place it in a separate method, which provides for more manageable code.

Handling Errors

There are three things you can do regarding any errors:

1. Don't handle them. In this case, the error will be silently eaten by the runtime.

2. Pass a second function to the *then* method. This function will be called if there was an error.

3. In custom screen methods, return the created **Promise** to the runtime (by placing the word *return* in front of the call to the **Promise**). The **LightSwitch** runtime attaches handlers for both erroneous and successful completion, and will show any errors that occurred to the user. It will also gray out the application and show a progress indicator if the **Promise** does not complete within a reasonable amount of time. This is the recommended approach for custom screen methods.

For Render Methods Use Binding

The best use of **Promise** methods is for external *async* calls. For **LightSwitch** data, you will still want to use data binding.

The **LightSwitch** team has made the following statement:

> *In render and post render code, you almost always want to use the data binding to handle cases where data is not loaded yet. By hooking up the data binding, the initial traversal of the data binding path will cause data to start loading and at some point later, your code will be called when the data has been loaded.*

For example, the following code **does not work**:

```
myapp.PromiseOrdersDetail.RowTemplate_render = function (element, contentItem) {

    // This does NOT work

        // Create a template
        var itemTemplate = $("<div></div>");

        // Get the Product name and quantity
        var ProductName = contentItem.value.PromiseProduct.ProductName;
        var ProductQuantity = contentItem.value.ProductQuantity;

        // Create the final display
        var FinalName = $("<h2>" + ProductName + ' [' + ProductQuantity + ']' + "</h2>");

        // Complete the template
        FinalName.appendTo($(itemTemplate));
        itemTemplate.appendTo($(element));
};
```

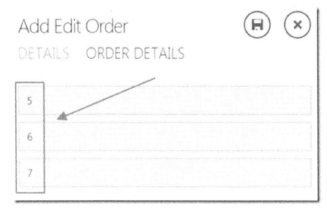

When we run the application, the associated **Products** have not had a chance to load, so the display is blank.

Instead, we use the following code that uses data binding:

```
myapp.AddEditPromiseOrders.RowTemplate_render = function (element, contentItem) {
    // We need to wait until the Products for the Order Detail are loaded
    // so we create a binding to "value.PromiseProduct.ProductName"
    // When the data is loaded the binding will be raised
    // We will then have all the data required for our display
    contentItem.dataBind("value.PromiseProduct.ProductName", function (newValue) {

        // Create a template
        var itemTemplate = $("<div></div>");

        // Get the Product name and quantity
        var ProductName = contentItem.value.PromiseProduct.ProductName;
        var ProductQuantity = contentItem.value.ProductQuantity;

        // Create the final display
        var FinalName = $("<h2>" + ProductName + ' [' + ProductQuantity + ']' + "</h2>");

        // Complete the template
        FinalName.appendTo($(itemTemplate));
        itemTemplate.appendTo($(element));

    });
};
```

Add Edit Order

DETAILS   ORDER DETAILS

Product One [2]

Product One [22]

The code now works as expected.

A **Promise** method could have been used, but it would not update when the values changed.

Chapter 4: Working With Data

The sample code for this chapter can be obtained at the links "Dynamically Creating Records In The LightSwitch HTML Client", "Deleting Data In The Visual Studio LightSwitch HTML Client", "Server Side Search using the LightSwitch HTML Client", and "Walk-thru Examples of Common Visual Studio LightSwitch JavaScript" at http://lightswitchhelpwebsite.com/Downloads.aspx

Most **LightSwitch** applications involve displaying, inserting, updating, and deleting data. This chapter will cover the things you need to know to manage data using the **LightSwitch HTML Client**.

Searching Data

The **LightSwitch HTML Client** allows you to easily create a server side search.

We start with a simple **Browse** screen.

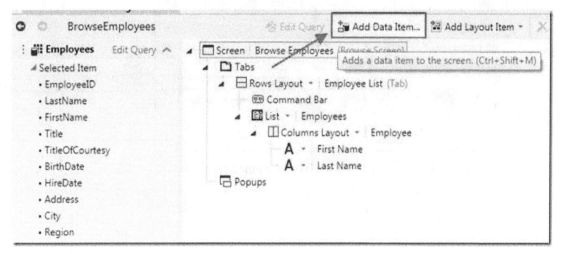

First, we add a property.

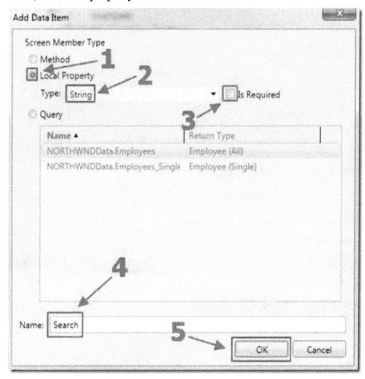

We create a **Search** property.

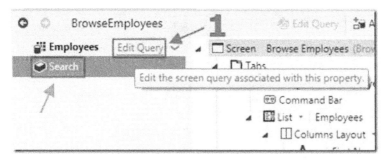

The property will be added to the **View Model** on the **Screen**.

We now select **Edit Query**.

We create a query that takes a **parameter**.

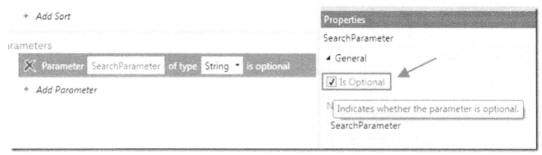

We click on the parameter, and in its **Properties,** we make it **Optional**.

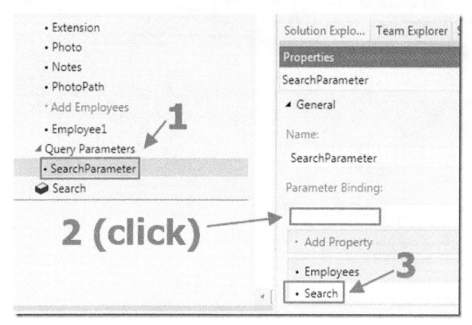

We bind the **Search** property to the **SearchParameter**.

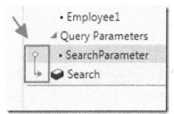

The line shows that the **Search** property is bound to the **SearchParameter**.

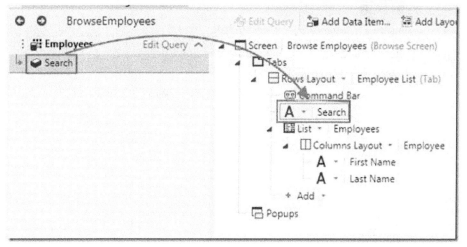

We drag and drop the **Search** property to the **Screen** layout.

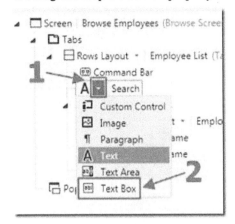

We switch the **Search** element to a **Text Box**.

When we run the application and enter a search term and hit the **Enter** key (or **Tab** or click away), a server side paged search is executed.

We can use the **F12** tools in the **Internet Explorer** web browser to see the data being transferred.

Setting Defaults

When you have a screen where the user creates a new record, you will usually want to set default values.

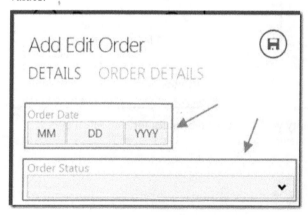

However, without custom **JavaScript**, default values will not be set.

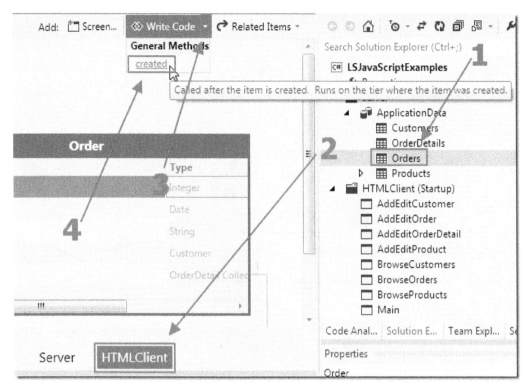

To set the default values, we open the entity we want to set the values for, and select the **HTMLClient** tab, and then the **created** method.

We use the following code:

```
myapp.Order.created = function (entity) {
    entity.OrderDate = new Date();
    entity.OrderStatus = 'New';
};
```

Dynamically Creating Records

You may have situations where you need to dynamically create records. Typically, you will want to do this when you don't want to navigate away to a new page to add a record.

Simple Example

For the simple example, we will show how to dynamically add a single simple **Entity**.

In this example, we will add a **Customer**.

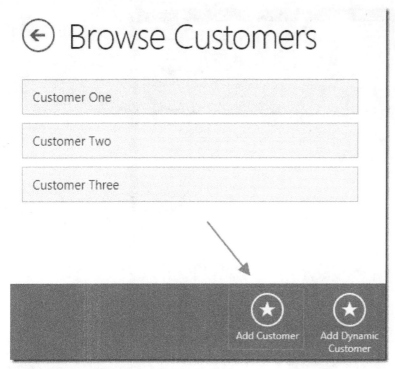

In the normal application program flow, we can start creating a record by clicking the **Add Customer** button.

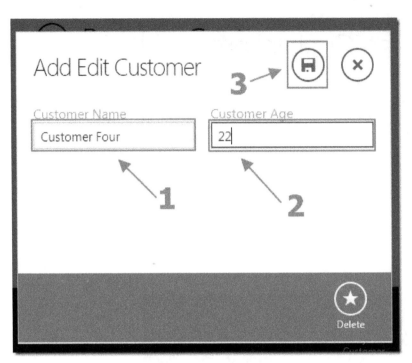

We add the **Customer** in the dialog that is displayed and click **Save**.

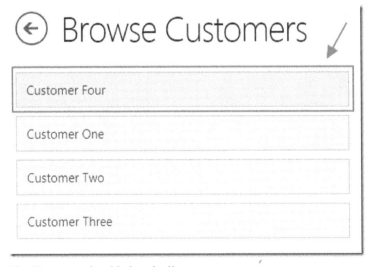

The **Customer** is added to the list.

However, if we click the **Add Dynamic Customer** button…

← Browse Customers

| New |
| Customer Four |
| Customer One |
| Customer Two |
| Customer Three |

★ Add Customer   ★ Add Dynamic Customer

...the **Customer** is added to the list immediately.

When we click on a record to edit it, or otherwise try to navigate away from the page, we will be asked to save the record.

We will also cover how to save the records immediately in the next section.

Creating the Simple Example

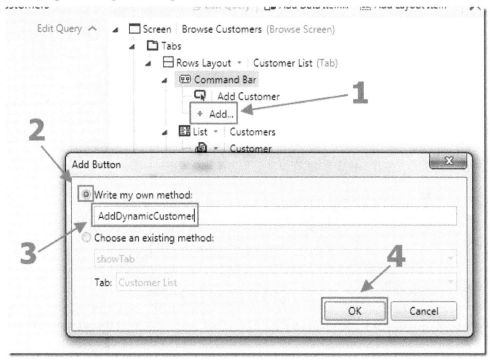

To create the code, we add a button to the screen and call it **AddDynamicCustomer**.

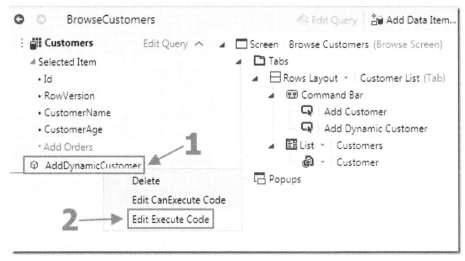

We *right-click* on the **AddDynamicCustomer** method in the **View Model**, and select the **Edit Execute Code** option.

We use the following code for the method:

```
myapp.BrowseCustomers.AddDynamicCustomer_execute = function (screen) {
    // Create a new Customer
    var newCustomer = new myapp.Customer();
    // Set the CustomerName
    newCustomer.CustomerName = "New";
    // Set the CustomerAge
    newCustomer.CustomerAge = 0;
};
```

Notice, if we wanted to save the records immediately, we would add the following code to the method:

```
// Save all changes on the screen
return myapp.activeDataWorkspace.ApplicationData
    .saveChanges().then(function () {
        // Refresh the Customers
        screen.getCustomers();
    });
```

Complex Example

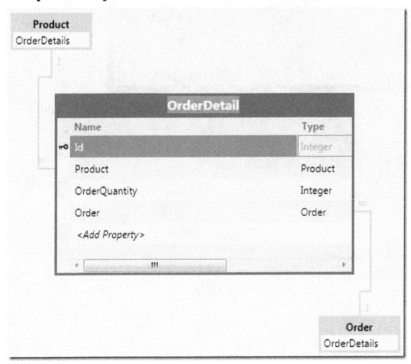

When a table (an **Entity**) has associated **Entities**, you have to perform a few extra steps. These extra steps may include searching a related **Entity** for a record to use as a default value.

In this example, we have an **OrderDetail Entity** that has associated **Order** and **Product Entities**.

In the normal application program flow, we can start creating a record by clicking the **Add Order Detail** button.

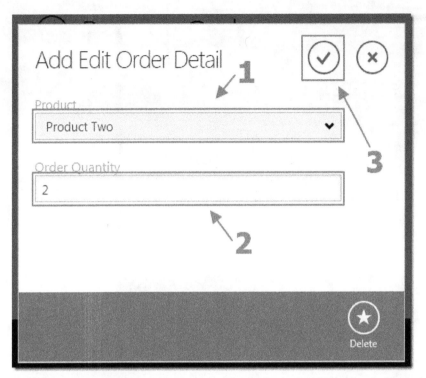

We select the **Product** and set the **Order Quantity** in the dialog that is displayed.

*The **Order** is also set, but it is not shown. **LightSwitch** knows what to set because we have associated the **Order Details** collection with an **Order** on the screen, and we are adding a record to that collection.*

Add Edit Order

DETAILS   ORDER DETAILS

2	Product Two
10	Product Three

Add Order Detail   Dynamic Add Order Detail

The **Order Detail** is added to the list.

However, if we click the **Dynamic Add Order Detail** button...

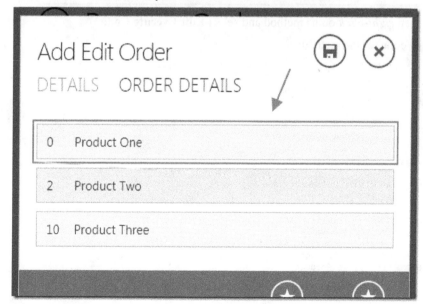

The **Order Detail** is added to the list immediately.

Creating the Complex Example

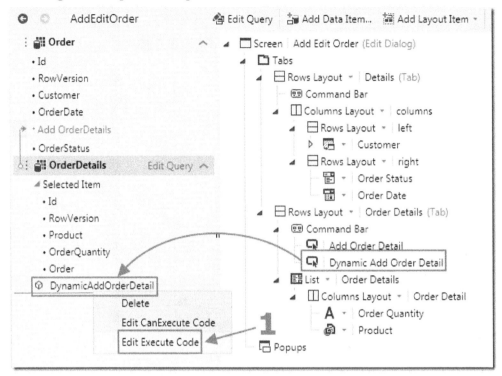

We create a button then *right-click* on its method and select **Edit Execute Code**.

We use the following code for the method:

```
myapp.AddEditOrder.DynamicAddOrderDetail_execute = function (screen) {
    // Make a new OrderDetail
    var newOrderDetail = new myapp.OrderDetail();
    // Set the Order property
    // Whenever you have associated Entities, there will
    // be a .set[Entity Name] method available
    newOrderDetail.setOrder(screen.Order);
    // Set the Quantity
    newOrderDetail.OrderQuantity = 0;
    // Try to find a Product
    var Products = screen.details.dataWorkspace.ApplicationData.Products
        .load().then(function (results) {
            // Try to get the first Product
            var FirstProduct = results.results[0];
            // Did we find a first Product?
            if (FirstProduct != undefined && FirstProduct != null) {
                // Set the first Product as the Product for the OrderDetail
                newOrderDetail.setProduct(FirstProduct);
            }
        });
}
```

Deleting Data

You have multiple options when you programmatically delete data in the **Visual Studio LightSwitch HTML Client**. Unlike the insert and update tasks, there is no wizard to easily create a button to allow a user to delete data. You must write a bit of code.

The second chapter of this book provides an example of the most common method.

The issue you may run into is what happens after the data is deleted. Do you want the user to stay on the page or automatically navigate away to the previous page?

The **LightSwitch API** methods that you will want to learn are:

- **commitChanges**
  - o Runs validation on the current active screen tab
  - o If there are no validation errors, it calls the data service saveChanges()
  - o Navigates back to previous screen

- **applyChanges**
  - o Runs validation on the current active screen tab
  - o If there are no validation errors, it calls the data service saveChanges()

- **cancelChanges**
  - o Invokes data service discardChanges()
  - o Navigates back to previous screen

- **discardChanges**
  - o Invokes data service discardChanges()
  - o The Sample Application

The sample application has three delete buttons on the **Browse Customers** screen. We have *restricted delete* enabled, so you cannot delete a **Customer** if that **Customer** has associated orders.

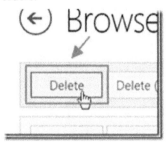

It has a normal **Delete** button. When you press it, nothing happens visually.

However, when you press a button to navigate away from the page…

…you are presented with a box to save or discard your changes.

If there are validation errors, they will show only if you select **Save Changes**.

The following code is used to implement this version:

```
myapp.BrowseCustomers.Delete_execute = function (screen) {
    screen.getCustomers().then(function (customers) {
        // Delete selected
        customers.deleteSelected();
    });
};
```

The following methods will explore alternative application flow scenarios.

commitChanges / cancelChanges

When we press the **Commit Changes** button…

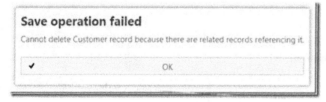

…if there are validation errors, they show at this point.

 Main

The user is then navigated to the previous page.

The following code is used to implement this version:

```
myapp.BrowseCustomers.CommitChanges_execute = function (screen) {
    screen.getCustomers().then(function (customers) {
        // Delete selected
        customers.deleteSelected();
        // Save changes
        myapp.commitChanges().then(null, function fail(e) {
            // If error occurs, show the error.
            msls.showMessageBox(e.message, { title: e.title }).then(function () {
                // Cancel Changes
                myapp.cancelChanges();
                throw e;
            });
        });
    });
};
```

applyChanges / discardChanges

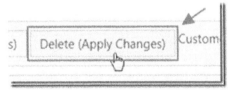

When we press the **Apply Changes** button…

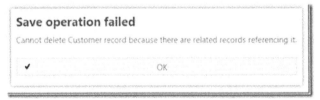

…if there are validation errors, they show at this point.

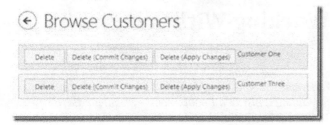

The user is **not** navigated away and remains on the page.

The following code is used to implement this version:

```
myapp.BrowseCustomers.ApplyChanges_execute = function (screen) {
    screen.getCustomers().then(function (customers) {
        // Delete selected
        customers.deleteSelected();
        // Save changes
        myapp.applyChanges().then(null, function fail(e) {
            // If error occurs, show the error.
            msls.showMessageBox(e.message, { title: e.title }).then(function () {
                // Discard Changes
                screen.details.dataWorkspace.ApplicationData
                    .details.discardChanges();
            });
        });
    });
};
```

Chapter 5: Working With Screens

The sample code for this chapter can be obtained at the links "Understanding The LightSwitch HTML Client Visual Collection", "Walk-thru Examples of Common Visual Studio LightSwitch JavaScript", "Programmatically Constraining a List In a Popup", and "Visual Studio LightSwitch Screen Navigation and Advanced JavaScript Examples" at http://lightswitchhelpwebsite.com/Downloads.aspx.

Some of the examples are based on the MSDN documentation, "How to: Modify an HTML Screen by Using Code" (http://bit.ly/11j2p91).

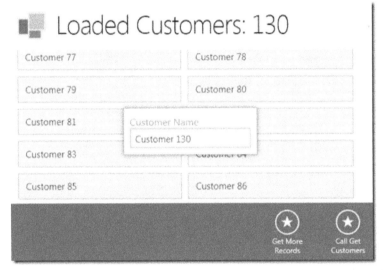

To maximize performance, all applications must properly manage the flow of data. When dealing with an entity (one row of data), **Visual Studio LightSwitch** transfers the entire entity from the data layer to the client, the user interface (UI) layer.

When dealing with collections (rows of data), **LightSwitch** uses **Visual Collections**, and it is very deliberate as to *how* and *when* it places entities in the **Visual Collection**.

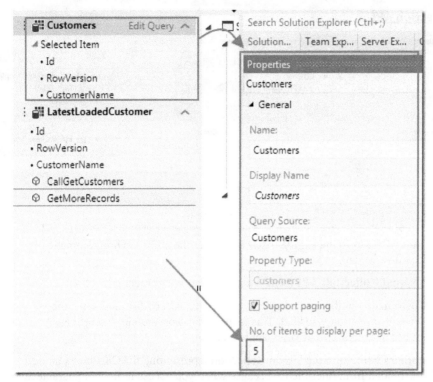

The key thing to note is **LightSwitch** will *page* the data. Meaning, it will not load all the data at one time. In our example, we have set the paging to 5 items at a time. However, when we run the application, it will typically display over 50 records when it starts.

/ApplicationData.svc/Customers?$skip=5&$top=5	GET	200	application/json	2.04 KB	110 ms
/ApplicationData.svc/Customers?$skip=10&$top=5	GET	200	application/json	2.06 KB	47 ms
/ApplicationData.svc/Customers?$skip=15&$top=5	GET	200	application/json	2.06 KB	109 ms
/ApplicationData.svc/Customers?$skip=20&$top=5	GET	200	application/json	2.06 KB	109 ms
/ApplicationData.svc/Customers?$skip=25&$top=5	GET	200	application/json	2.06 KB	78 ms
/ApplicationData.svc/Customers?$skip=30&$top=5	GET	200	application/json	2.06 KB	78 ms
/ApplicationData.svc/Customers?$skip=35&$top=5	GET	200	application/json	2.06 KB	63 ms
/ApplicationData.svc/Customers?$skip=40&$top=5	GET	200	application/json	2.06 KB	78 ms
/ApplicationData.svc/Customers?$skip=45&$top=5	GET	200	application/json	2.06 KB	78 ms
/ApplicationData.svc/Customers?$skip=50&$top=5	GET	200	application/json	2.06 KB	63 ms
/ApplicationData.svc/Customers?$skip=55&$top=5	GET	200	application/json	2.06 KB	156 ms
/ApplicationData.svc/Customers?$skip=60&$top=5	GET	200	application/json	2.06 KB	93 ms

When we do a network trace of the running application, we see it makes multiple requests, *5 records* at a time.

The Visual Collection API

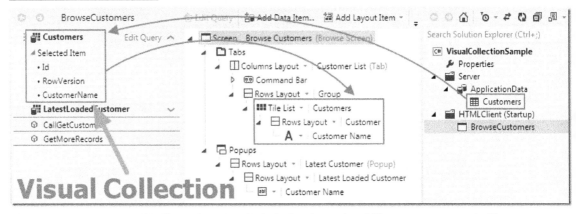

The **Visual Collection API** allows the **LightSwitch** developer the ability to programmatically detect and manage the flow of data.

We will look at the **Visual Collection API** using a hypothetical **Customers** collection:

- **screen.getCustomers()** will return a Promise object that will be fulfilled when the Customers Visual Collection is loaded. This is the one exposed under IntelliSense because most of the time it's what you want to use.

- **screen.Customers** will return the Visual Collection representing the Customers on the screen. This is hidden from IntelliSense because when you access it, it's not guaranteed the Visual Collection is loaded. But it's useful to set up change listener.

- **screen.Customers.data** will return an array of all Customers loaded into the Visual Collection.

- **screen.Customer.selectedItem** will return the currently selected Customer in the Visual Collection.

screen.getCustomers() and screen.Customers.data

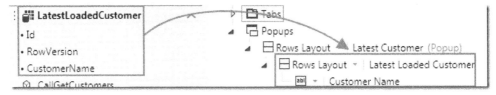

This first example will look at the **.get** method that returns a **Promise** object for the collection.

This example will also show how we can iterate through the entities returned by the **Promise** object using the **.data** property.

To set up the example, we add a **Customer** entity (a single **Customer**) to the **View Model**. We will call it **LatestLoadedCustomer** (right now it is just empty). We create a **Popup,** and we drag the **LatestLoadedCustomer** entity to the **Popup**, so it will show when we open the **Popup**.

We create a button and use the following code:

```
myapp.BrowseCustomers.CallGetCustomers_execute = function (screen) {
    // Call getCustomers
    screen.getCustomers().then(function (result) {
        var index = result.data.length; // gets length of the full Customer array
        // The last Customer found in the
        // collection will be
        // set to LatestLoadedCustomer
        screen.LatestLoadedCustomer = result.data[index - 1]; // compensate for 0-based index
        // Show the Popup to display
        // LatestLoadedCustomer
        screen.showPopup("LatestCustomer");
    });
};
```

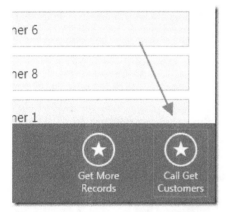

Then we run the application, and click the **Call Get Customers** button.

The last record retrieved by the method is displayed.
```
```

screen.Customers

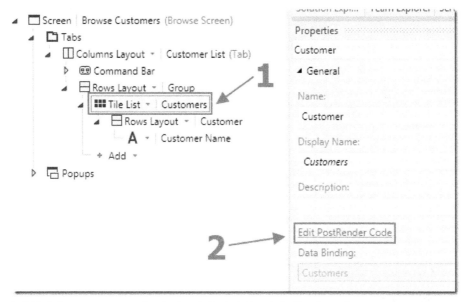

While it is not guaranteed to be loaded, the **Visual Collection** allows us to easily attach handlers, so our code will run *when* the **Visual Collection** *is* loaded with data.

In this example, we click on the **Tile List** that is bound to the **Customer** collection, and select **Edit PostRender Code**.

We use the following code:

```
myapp.BrowseCustomers.Customer_postRender = function (element, contentItem) {
    // Set up a databind on screen.Customers.count
    contentItem.dataBind("screen.Customers.count", function (newValue) {
        // Update the total records display
        DisplayCustomerCount(contentItem.screen);
    });
};
// Utility
function DisplayCustomerCount(screen) {
    // If there is a Customer collection
    // display the current count
    if (screen.Customers != undefined && screen.Customers != null) {
        var strDisplayText = "Loaded Customers: " + screen.Customers.count;
        screen.details.displayName = strDisplayText;
    }
}
```

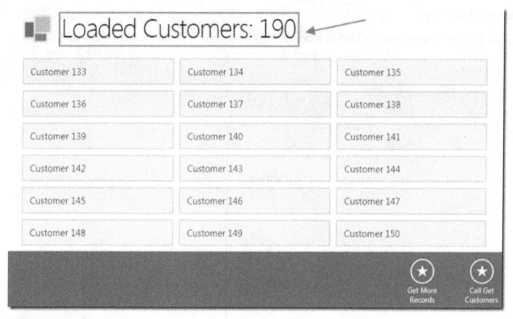

When we run the application, the number of loaded **Customers** will display.

We can also add the following code to the method:

```
// Set up a databind on screen.Customers.selectedItem
contentItem.dataBind("screen.Customers.selectedItem", function (newValue) {
    var SelectedItem = newValue;
    // do we have a selected Customer?
    if (SelectedItem != undefined && SelectedItem != null) {
        // Update the display to show the last selected Customer
        var strDisplayText = "SelectedItem CustomerName: " + SelectedItem.CustomerName;
        contentItem.screen.details.displayName = strDisplayText;
    }
});
```

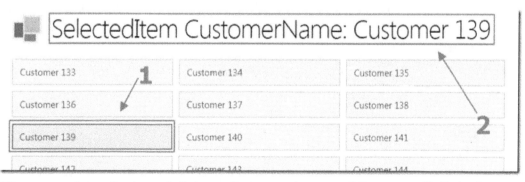

When we run the application and click on a **Customer**, the name of **Customer** will display in the title.

Manual Paging

In the previous examples, we loaded more records by scrolling down through the **Tile List**. We can also programmatically control the paging by manually loading records into the **Visual Collection**.

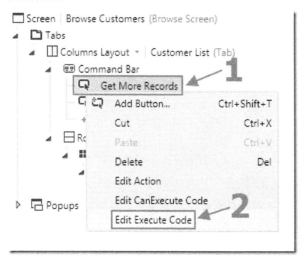

We create a button and use the following code:

```
myapp.BrowseCustomers.GetMoreRecords_execute = function (screen) {
    if (screen.Customers.canLoadMore) {
        // We can load more records -- load them
        screen.Customers.loadMore().then(function (result) {
            var index = result.items.length; // gets length of the full Customer array
            // The last Customer found in the
            // collection will be
            // set to LatestLoadedCustomer
            screen.LatestLoadedCustomer = result.items[index - 1]; // compensate for 0-based index
            // Show the Popup to display
            // LatestLoadedCustomer
            screen.showPopup("LatestCustomer");
            // Update the total records display
            DisplayCustomerCount(screen);
        });
    }
};
```

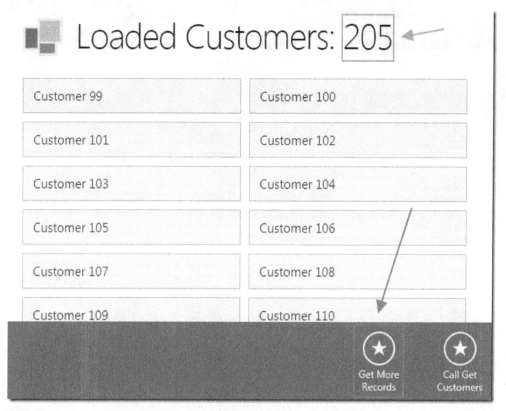

Loaded Customers: 205

Customer 99	Customer 100
Customer 101	Customer 102
Customer 103	Customer 104
Customer 105	Customer 106
Customer 107	Customer 108
Customer 109	Customer 110

Get More Records

Call Get Customers

When we run the application, we can click the **Get More Records** button.

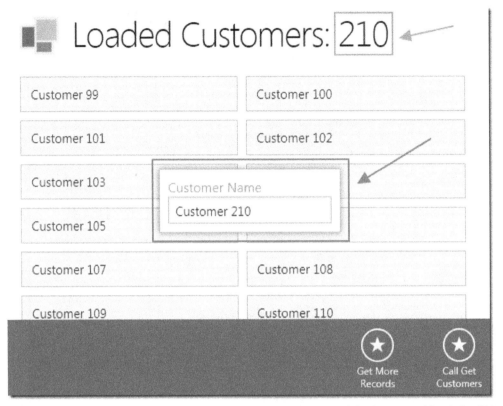

Additional records will be loaded into the **Visual Collection**, and the last record loaded will be displayed.

JavaScript

We will now look at some examples that demonstrate how **JavaScript** can be used to programmatically manage the screen.

Format a Number

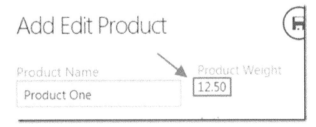

LightSwitch contains many controls to format values such as dates and currencies. However, sometimes you need to show special formats, such as a number that needs to show two digits after the decimal.

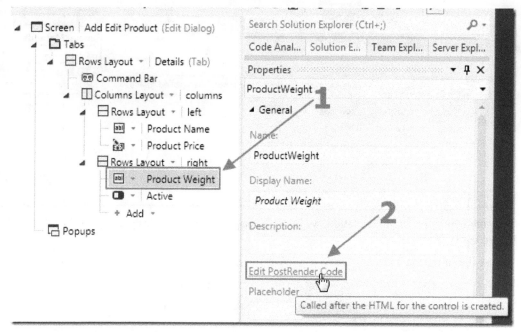

To implement our custom formatting, we open the page in the screen designer, select the control, and select **Edit PostRender Code**.

We use the following code:

```
myapp.AddEditProduct.ProductWeight_postRender = function (element, contentItem) {
    contentItem.dataBind("value", function (value) {
        if (value) {
            $(element).text(value.toFixed(2));
        }
    });
};
```

Validate Data on a Screen

LightSwitch automatically provides validation for most situations. For example, if you have an integer field and the user enters string characters, **LightSwitch** will automatically show validation errors when the user attempts to save.

However, sometimes you require custom validation.

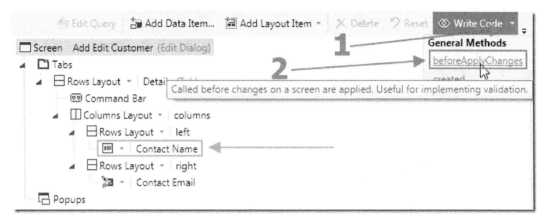

To implement our custom validation, we open the page in the screen designer, and select **beforeApplyChanges**.

We use the following code:

```
myapp.AddEditCustomer.beforeApplyChanges = function (screen) {
    if (screen.Customer.ContactName.indexOf('!') != -1) {
        screen.findContentItem("ContactName").validationResults = [
        new msls.ValidationResult(
        screen.Customer.details.properties.ContactName,
        "Contact Name cannot contain the character '!'.")
        ];
        return false;
    }
};
```

The validation will show when we run the application:

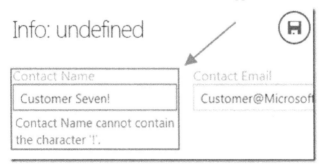

Set the Screen Title Dynamically

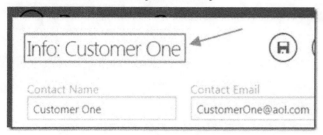

JavaScript is required to programmatically set the title of a screen.

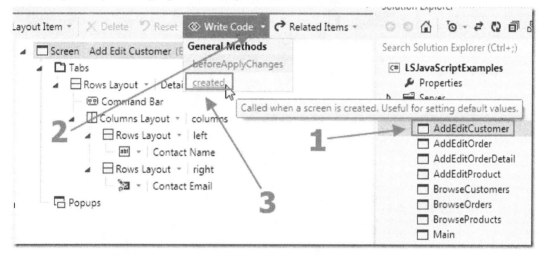

We open the screen in the screen designer, and select the **created** method.

We use the following code for the method:

```
myapp.AddEditCustomer.created = function (screen) {
    // Set the screen title dynamically
    var name;
    name = screen.Customer.ContactName;
    screen.details.displayName = "Info: " + name;
};
```

Disable a Button

You may have a need to programmatically disable a button.

In the screen designer, we add a button.

We name the button *DisabledButton*.

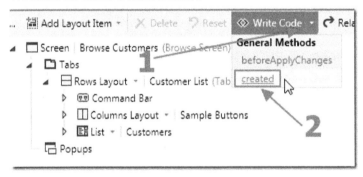

We select the **created** method for the screen.

We use the following code for the method:

```
myapp.BrowseCustomers.created = function (screen) {
    // Find DisabledButton and disable it
    screen.findContentItem("DisabledButton").isEnabled = false;
};
```

Render HTML Directly On a Screen

← The name of this page is Main

You can render HTML markup directly on the screen. In this example, we will use the HTML **marquee** tag to display a scrolling message.

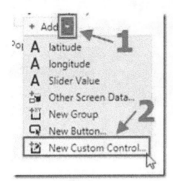

In the screen designer, we add a **Custom Control**.

Use the default value of *Screen* for the data binding.

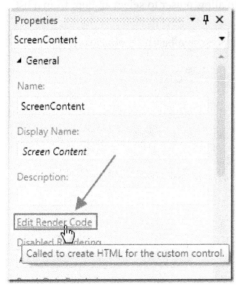

In the **Properties** for the control, we select **Edit Render Code** and use the following code:

```
myapp.Main.ScreenContent_render = function (element, contentItem) {
    //Get the name of the page
    var pageName = contentItem.screen.details.displayName;
    element.innerHTML = '<marquee>The name of this page is ' + pageName + '</marquee>';
};
```

Programmatically Constraining a List in a Popup

LightSwitch will allow you to easily create a popup to allow a user to select an item from a list in an associated table and to set a value.

What is more difficult is constraining that list of items presented based on business rules.

The Sample Application

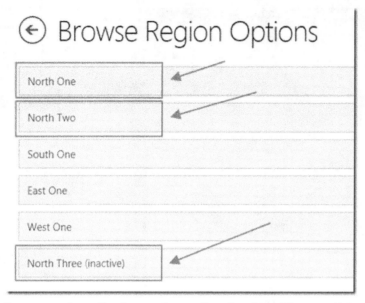

In our sample application, we have a list of **regions**. There are three in the **North**. One of the items is *inactive*.

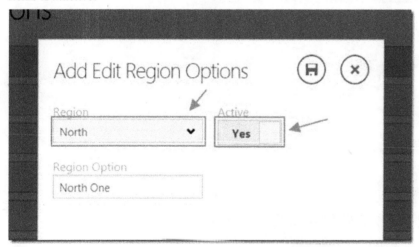

When we click on a **region record,** we can select the **region** (North, South, East, or West) and give the **region option** a name.

We can also indicate if the **region** is *active* (or not).

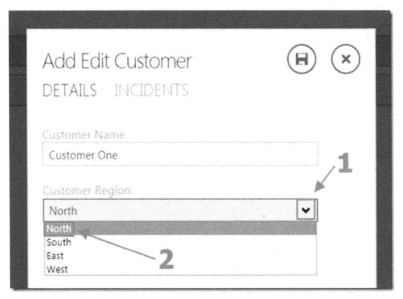

When we edit a **Customer,** we can set their **region**.

We will now look at the constrained list in the Popup.

We can add **Incidents** for a **Customer**.

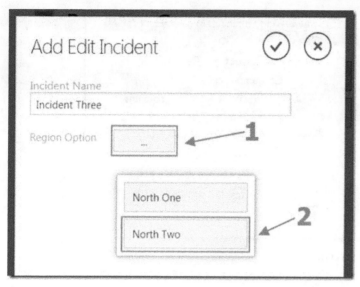

When we click the button to set the **region option** for the **Customer**, we only see *active* **region options** for the region the **Customer** is in.

When we select a **region option** in the **Popup**, it is set as the **region option** for the **Incident**.

Creating the Application

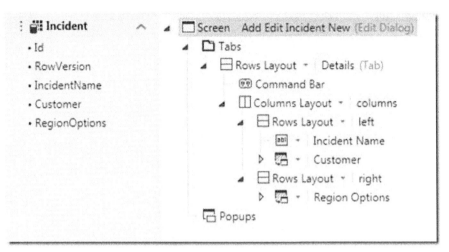

We create a normal **Add/Edit screen**.

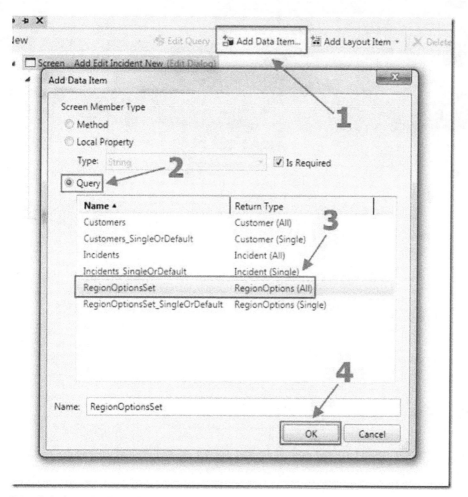

We click the **Add Data Item** button, and add the **RegionOptions** collection.

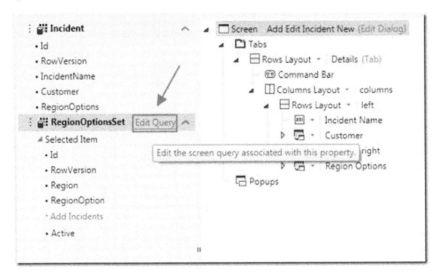

We click **Edit Query** on the collection.

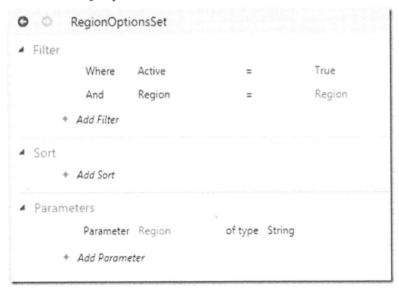

We create a query to implement our business rules.

We also create a **Region** parameter for the query.

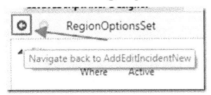

We click the **Back** button to return to the screen designer.

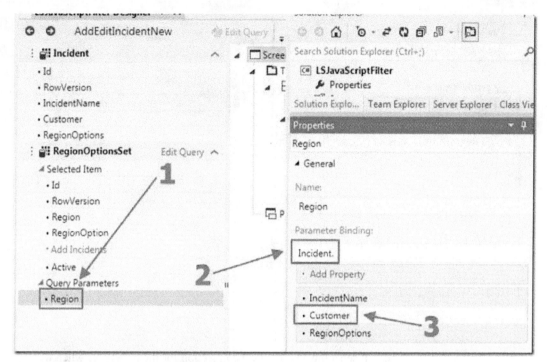

We specify the value for our parameter by clicking on it, and in the **Properties**, navigate to the **Customer** property of the **Incident** entity.

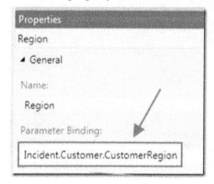

We select the **CustomerRegion** of the **Customer** entity.

This will constrain the list to show only the **Region Options** the **Customer** (for the related **Incident**) is in.

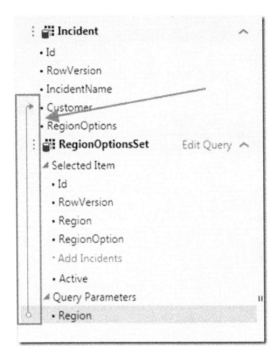

In the screen designer, we will see a line showing the connection for the parameter when we click on it.

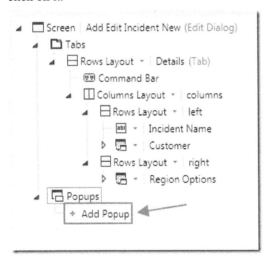

Next, we add a **Popup**.

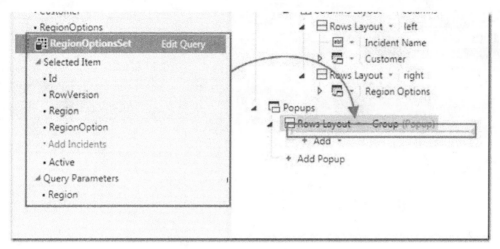

We drag and drop the **RegionOptions** collection onto the **Popup**.

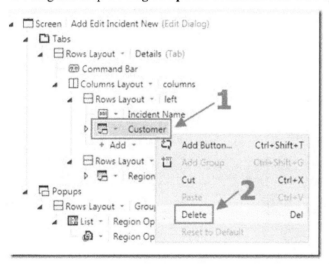

We delete the **Customer** selection control. It is not needed because a **Customer** has already been selected for the **Incident** by the time we get to this screen.

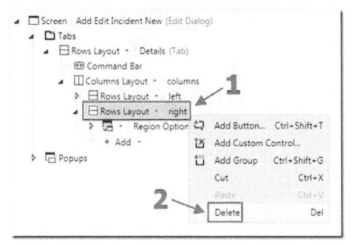

We also delete the second column on the first tab because it is not needed.

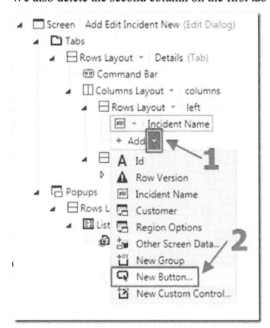

We add a new **Button**.

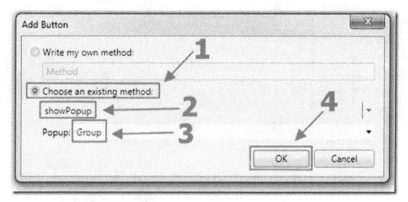

We set it to open the **Popup**.

We set "**...**" as the display name for the **Popup**.

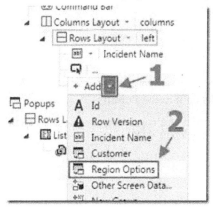

We add the **Region Options** control to the first tab.

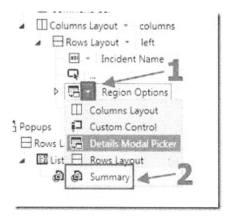

We change the **Region Options** control to only display the **Summary**.

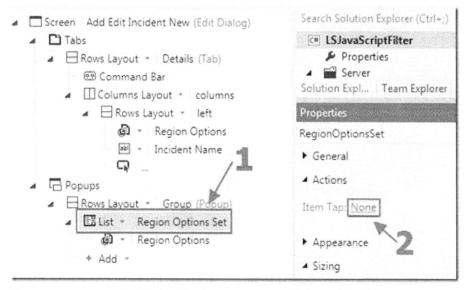

Now, we want to set the **Region Option** when a user clicks on it in the **Popup**.

We click on the **Region Options Set List** in the **Popup**, and in its **Properties**, we click the **Item Tap** action.

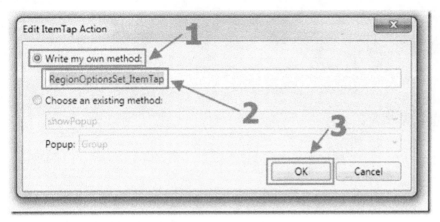

We create a method for the **Action**.

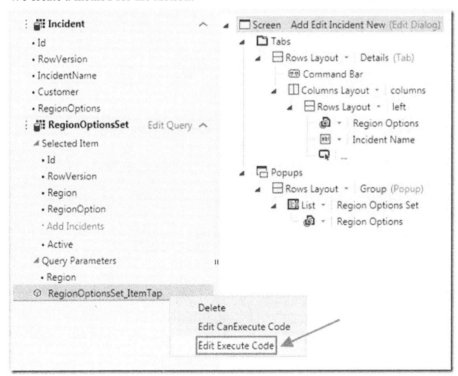

Next, we *right-click* on the newly created method in the **View Model** and select the **Edit Execute Code** option.

We use the following code for the method:

```
myapp.AddEditIncidentNew.RegionOptionsSet_ItemTap_execute = function (screen) {
    // Get the list that is in the Popup
    var RegionOptionsSet = screen.findContentItem("RegionOptionsSet");
    // Get the selected item in the list
    var RegionOption = RegionOptionsSet.value.selectedItem;
    // update Region for the Incident
    screen.Incident.setRegionOptions(RegionOption);
    //Close the Popup
    screen.closePopup();
};
```

Simple Method

If you need to add additional items to the **Popup**, such as a search within the list shown on the **Popup**, the previous method will work.

However, if a simple list is all you require, you don't actually need to create the **Popup** or write any code.

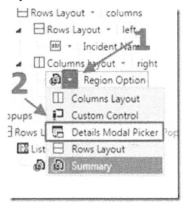

We change the **Region Option** control to a **Details Modal Picker**.

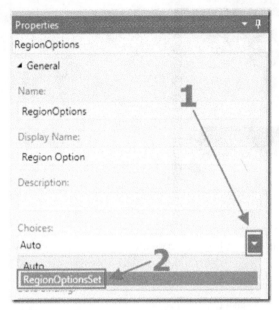

In the **Properties** for the **Modal Picker**, we change the **Choices** to the **RegionOptions** collection, which contains the query that implements the business rules.

When we run the program, a drop down appears that causes a **Popup** to show.

Changing the Color of List Boxes

This example demonstrates how to easily apply **CSS** style to a **List**.

In this example, we have code that will show an item in **blue** if the quantity is over 5 and **yellow** if it is 5 or less.

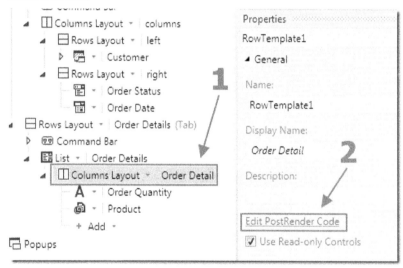

To create the code, we click on the **Layout** control and click the **Edit PostRender Code** link in the **Properties**.

We use the following code for the method:

```
// Value to hold the cached OrderDetailRowParent
var OrderDetailRowParent;
myapp.AddEditOrder.RowTemplate1_postRender = function (element, contentItem) {
    // Cache the OrderDetail item so it can possibly be updated
    OrderDetailRowParent = $(element).parent();
    // Get Order Quantity
    var OrderQuantity = contentItem.data.OrderQuantity;
    if (OrderQuantity != null && OrderQuantity != undefined) {
        // If we have a value -- color the line item
        ColorOrderDetail(OrderQuantity);
    }
};
// Utility
function ColorOrderDetail(OrderQuantity) {
    // if OrderQuantity is more than 5 make the background Blue
    // otherwise make it Yellow
    if (OrderQuantity > 5) {
        OrderDetailRowParent.css({
            "background-color": "blue",
            "background-image": "none",
            color: "white"
        });
    }
    else {
        OrderDetailRowParent.css({
            "background-color": "yellow",
            "background-image": "none",
            color: "black"
        });
    }
}
```

However, if we create a **new** record, there is no coloring applied.

We can resolve this by **caching** an object, so it can be updated later.

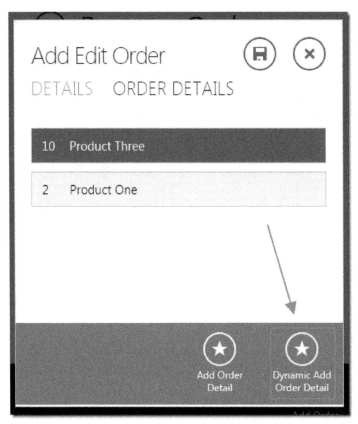

First, let's see how the completed example works.

When we click the **Dynamic Add Order Detail** button…

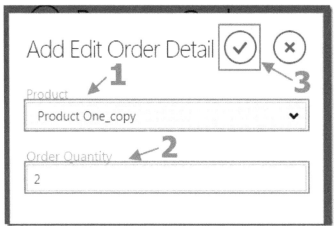

…the **Add Edit Order Detail** screen opens and allows us to enter the details.

We click the **Check** button to accept the edit.

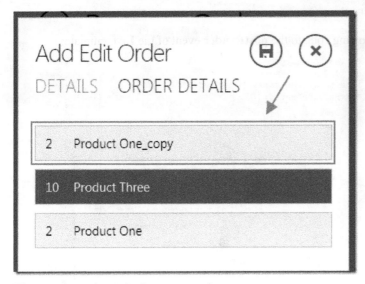

The new item shows in the proper color.

The following code is used for the button:

```
// Value to hold the cached OrderDetailRowParent
var OrderDetailRowParent;
myapp.AddEditOrder.DynamicAddOrderDetail_execute = function (screen) {
    myapp.showAddEditOrderDetail(null, {
        beforeShown: function (AddEditOrderDetailScreen) {
            // Make a new OrderDetail
            var newOrderDetail = new myapp.OrderDetail();
            // Set the Order property
            newOrderDetail.setOrder(screen.Order);
            // Set the Quantity
            newOrderDetail.OrderQuantity = 0;
            // Try to find a Product
            screen.details.dataWorkspace.ApplicationData.Products
                .load().then(function (results) {
                    // Try to get the first Product
                    var FirstProduct = results.results[0];
                    // Did we find a first Product?
                    if (FirstProduct != undefined && FirstProduct != null) {
                        // Set the first Product as the Product for the OrderDetail
                        newOrderDetail.setProduct(FirstProduct);
                    }
                    AddEditOrderDetailScreen.OrderDetail = newOrderDetail;
                });
        },
        afterClosed: function (AddEditOrderDetailScreen, navigationAction) {
            // Update the last cached OrderDetailRowParent item
            ColorOrderDetail(AddEditOrderDetailScreen.OrderDetail.OrderQuantity);
        }
    });
};
```

However, if we **update** an existing record, there is no coloring applied.

We can resolve this by adding a **click event** to the **cached** item.

The first step is to add the following code to the **postRender** event of the **List** template:

```
// Update the cached order when one is selected
$(element).on("click", function () {
    // Cache the OrderDetail item so it can possibly be updated
    OrderDetailRowParent = $(element).parent();
});
```

Next, we create our own event that will be fired when the **List** control is clicked on.

We use the following code for its method:

```
myapp.AddEditOrder.DynamicEditOrderDetail_execute = function (screen) {
    // Open the AddEditOrderDetail screen
    // Passing it the currently selected OrderDetails item
    myapp.showAddEditOrderDetail(screen.OrderDetails.selectedItem, {
        afterClosed: function (AddEditOrderDetailScreen, navigationAction) {
            // Update the last cached OrderDetailRowParent item
            ColorOrderDetail(AddEditOrderDetailScreen.OrderDetail.OrderQuantity);
        }
    });
};
```

Chapter 6: Application Navigation

The sample code for this chapter can be obtained at the links "Walk-thru Examples of Common Visual Studio LightSwitch JavaScript", "Visual Studio LightSwitch Screen Navigation and Advanced JavaScript Examples", and "HUY Volume II - Visual Studio LightSwitch Advanced JavaScript Examples" at http://lightswitchhelpwebsite.com/Downloads.aspx.

Some of the examples are based on the MSDN documentation, "How to: Modify an HTML Screen by Using Code" (http://bit.ly/11j2p91).

The following sections describe solutions to common situations regarding application navigation.

Show a Message Box, and Respond To a User Selection

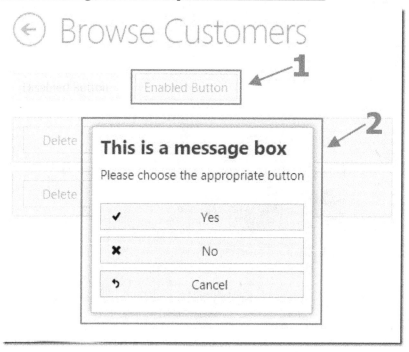

Sometimes we desire to show a message box.

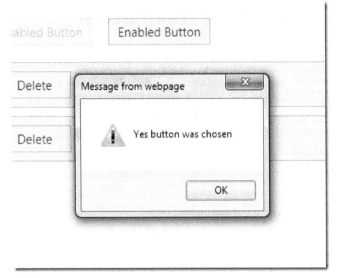

We also desire to respond to user input.

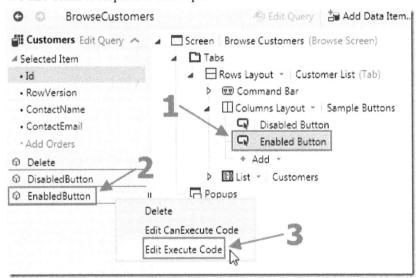

To implement the message box, we add a button to the screen in the screen designer.

We **right-click** on the method for the button and use the following code:

```
myapp.BrowseCustomers.EnabledButton_execute = function (screen) {
    msls.showMessageBox("Please choose the appropriate button", {
        title: "This is a message box",
        buttons: msls.MessageBoxButtons.yesNoCancel
    })
        .then(function (result) {
        if (result === msls.MessageBoxResult.yes) {
            alert("Yes button was chosen");
        }
        else if (result === msls.MessageBoxResult.no) {
            alert("No button was chosen");
        }
        else if (result === msls.MessageBoxResult.cancel) {
            alert("Please choose either Yes or No");
        }
    });
};
```

Create a Custom Modal Picker by Using A Popup

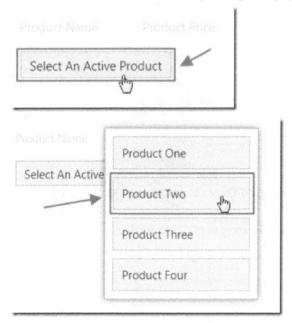

LightSwitch will automatically create popups that allow you to choose a value from a collection. However, you may have a situation where you want to control the choices in the popup.

In our sample, we have set a **Product** to not be active. We do not want it to show as an option in the popup.

We *right-click* on the **Products** table and select **Add Query** to create a new query called **ActiveProducts**.

We create the query to only show *Active* **Products** using the following criteria:

Next, we add the query to the screen.

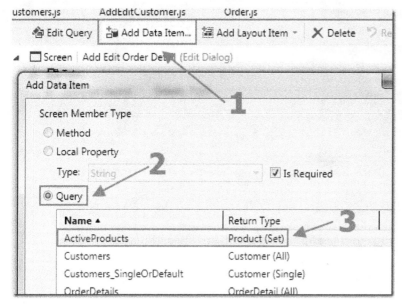

In the screen designer, we select **Add Data Item**, **Query**, and then select **ActiveProducts**.

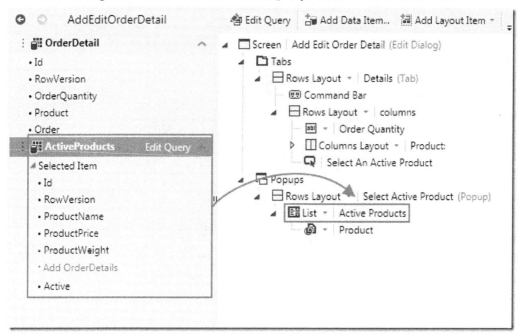

We click on the **Popups** node in the screen designer and select **Add Popup**.

We add the **ActiveProducts** collection to a popup by dragging and dropping it on the popup.

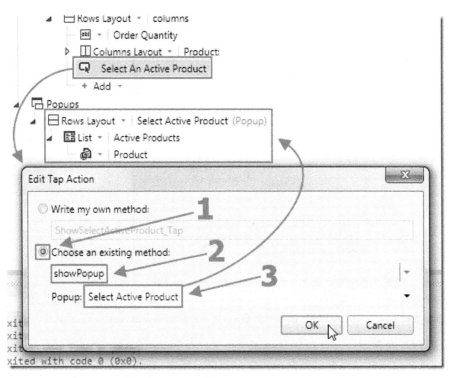

We create a button and set it to open the popup.

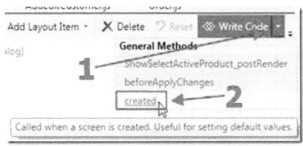

We select the **created** method for the screen and use the following code for the method:

```
myapp.AddEditOrderDetail.created = function (screen) {
    screen.findContentItem("ActiveProducts")
        .dataBind("value.selectedItem", function (newValue) {
        if (newValue !== undefined && newValue !== null) {
            //Whenever selectedItem for Products changes,
            // update the Product value on the main page
            screen.OrderDetail.setProduct(newValue);
            //Close popup, if one is open.
            screen.closePopup();
        }
    });
};
```

Copy a Record - Show Add Edit Dialog with Initialized Parameters

A very powerful tool is the **beforeShown** option that allows us to create default values for a screen we are opening from another screen.

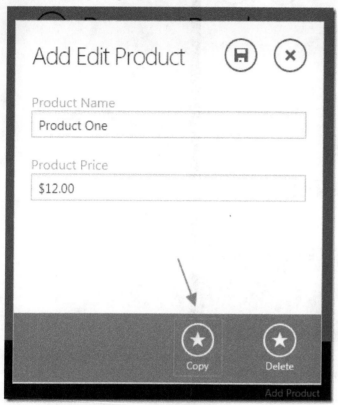

In this example, we will use it to implement a **Copy** button on an edit screen.

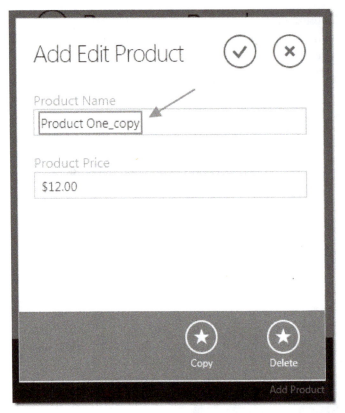

When you click the **Copy** button, it opens another screen, copies the contents of the previous screen, and appends the text _copy to the **Product Name**.

Click the **Check** button to accept the change.

This returns you to the previous screen where you can now click the **Save** button.

Both records are now saved.

Creating the Example

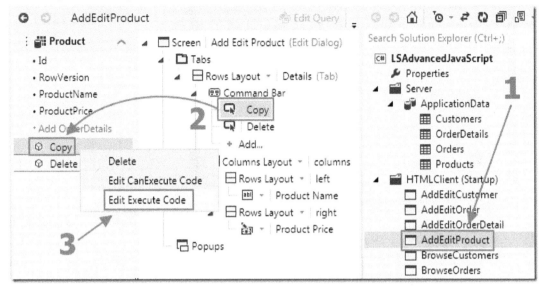

To create the code, we open the **AddEditProduct** screen and add a **Copy** button.

We then *right-click* on the method for the button in the **View Model** and select **Edit Execute Code**.

We use the following code for the button:

```
myapp.AddEditProduct.Copy_execute = function (screen) {
    myapp.showAddEditProduct(null, {
        beforeShown: function (addNewScreen) {
            var copied_item = screen.Product;
            var new_item = new myapp.Product();
            new_item.ProductName = copied_item.ProductName + '_copy';
            new_item.ProductPrice = copied_item.ProductPrice;
            // Set Product
            addNewScreen.Product = new_item;
        }
    });
};
```

Note: With the show method, be aware that depending on the particular page, the method may take different parameters than the ones in this example. You can us IntelliSense to determine what parameters the method expects.

Navigating to a New Screen (and Returning)

Another very powerful tool is the **afterClosed** option, which allows us to indicate what happens when we return from a screen we opened.

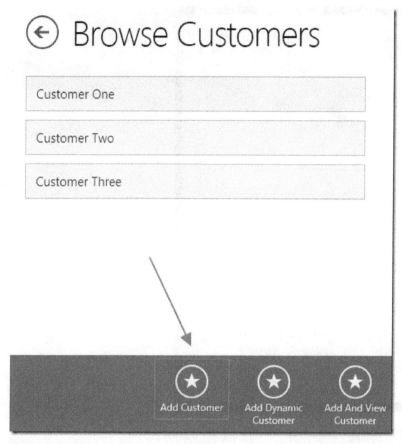

The normal program flow for creating a new **Customer** record is to first click the **Add Customer** button.

The **Add Edit** screen shows.

We enter information and click the **Save** button.

We are navigated back to the **Browse Customer** screen and the new record displays.

Now, let us look at an alternative flow. When we click the **Add And View Customer** button...

...the same **Add Edit** screen opens. However, when we click **Save**...

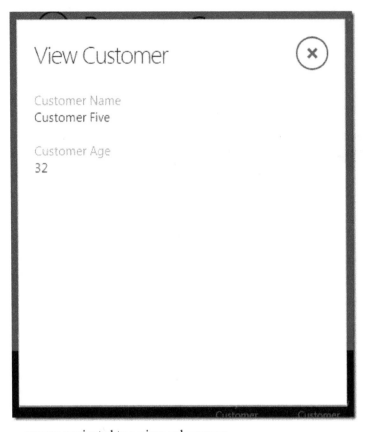

...we are navigated to a view only screen.

This happens because we used the **afterClose** option in the code for the button.

The following code is used for the **Add And View Customer** button:

```
myapp.BrowseCustomers.AddAndViewCustomer_execute = function (screen) {
    myapp.showAddEditCustomer(null, {
        beforeShown: function (addEditScreen) {
            // Create new Customer here so that
            // discard will work.
            var newCustomer = new myapp.Customer();
            addEditScreen.Customer = newCustomer;
        },
        afterClosed: function (addEditScreen, navigationAction) {
            // If the user commits the change,
            // show the new Customer in View Screen.
            if (navigationAction === msls.NavigateBackAction.commit) {
                var newCustomer = addEditScreen.Customer;
                myapp.showViewCustomer(newCustomer);
            }
        }
    });
};
```

After Editing -- Return Focus and Browser Position to the Item

In our next example, we will show how you can return a user to the last position in a **List** after navigating away to edit an item in that **List**.

To implement this, we must first create a custom method to open the edit screen, rather than using the normal **LightSwitch** navigation wizard to create a button.

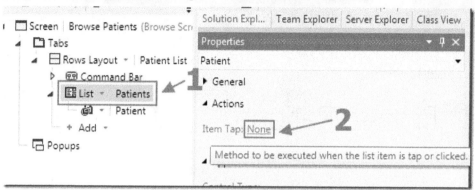

We click on the **List** and select **Item Tap** in the **Properties** for the **List**.

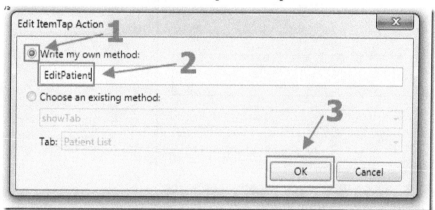

We select **Write my own method**, and enter **EditPatient** for the method name.

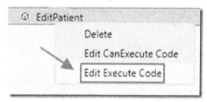

The method will show in the **View Model** on the screen designer.

Now, we *right-click* on the method, and then we select the **Edit Execute Code** option.

We use the following code for the method:

```
myapp.BrowsePatients.EditPatient_execute = function (screen) {
    // Set the scrollTopPosition
    var scrollTopPosition = $(window).scrollTop();
    // Open the Edit Screen
    myapp.showAddEditPatient(screen.Patients.selectedItem, {
        afterClosed: function () {
            // After the Edit screen is closed
            // scroll to the saved scrollTopPosition
            $(window).scrollTop(scrollTopPosition);
        }
    });
};
```

When we run the application…

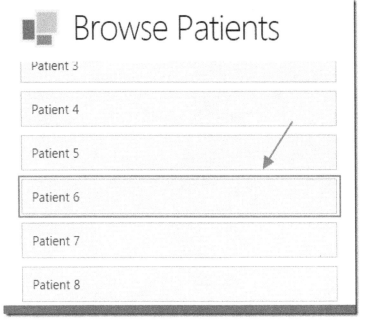

…we can scroll to a position in the list and click on an item to edit it.

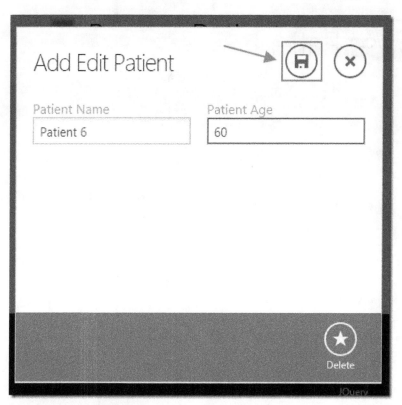

The edit screen will display.

We can edit the item and **Save** or **Close** the edit screen.

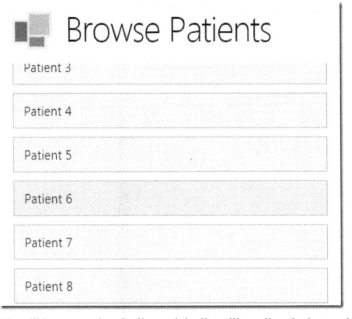

We will be returned to the list, and the list will scroll to the last position, rather than the default behavior of scrolling to the top of the list.

Chapter 7: Advanced Topics

Over the past year I have created more than 30 **Visual Studio LightSwitch HTML Client** projects. While creating those projects, I ran into challenges that required me to go deeper into the **LightSwitch HTML Client API**. The following sections cover the use of advanced techniques that I consider important to know.

Using ServerApplicationContext

The sample code for this section can be obtained at the links "Retrieving The Current User In The LightSwitch HTML Client", "Automatic Save (And Refresh)", "Full Control LightSwitch (ServerApplicationContext And Generic File Handlers And Ajax Calls)", and "Creating ASP.NET Web Forms CRUD Pages Using ServerApplicationContext" at http://lightswitchhelpwebsite.com/Downloads.aspx.

The **Visual Studio LightSwitch HTML Client** has a lot of built-in features. However, sometimes those features require you to structure your pages in the *LightSwitch way*. While this may work in most cases, sometimes it doesn't.

The **ServerApplicationContext** API allows your server-side code access to the **LightSwitch** middle-tier's data workspace. You can implement any functionality you need when you use **ServerApplicationContext, Generic File Handlers** (.ashx files), and **JQuery Ajax** calls.

Using this technique has the following additional benefits:

- The majority of the code is implemented in **ASP.NET** code that will show compile-time errors if you, for example, change the schema of a table.

- You have full control over the structure and organization of the code to assist in the management of a large code base.

Retrieving the Current User

In the **Visual Studio LightSwitch HTML Client**, extra steps are required to determine who the currently logged in user is.

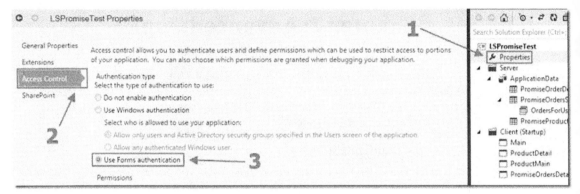

The first step is to turn on authentication in the **LightSwitch** project.

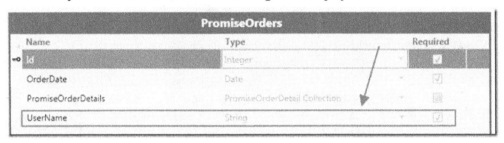

We create a **UserName** field. Notice it is *Required*.

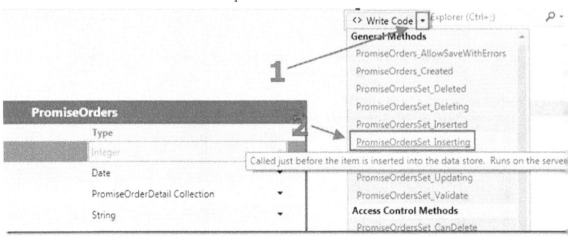

We select the **Entity** (table). Then we select **Write Code** and the *Inserting* method.

We use the following code for the method:

```
partial void PromiseOrdersSet_Inserting(PromiseOrders entity)
{
    // Set the Username
    entity.UserName = this.Application.User.Name;
}
```

We also set the updating method:

```
partial void PromiseOrdersSet_Updating(PromiseOrders entity)
{
    // Set the Username
    entity.UserName = this.Application.User.Name;
}
```

We need to do this to protect the **OData** service points. Setting this value only in the *client-side* code (shown later) is not enough. A user can access the **OData** service point directly and alter the value. Using the code above prevents this.

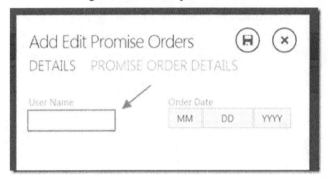

However, the **UserName** is not populated when we run the application.

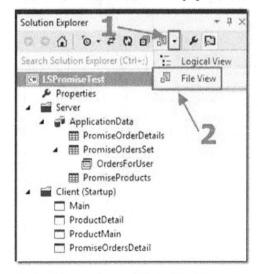

To fix this, we first switch to **File View**.

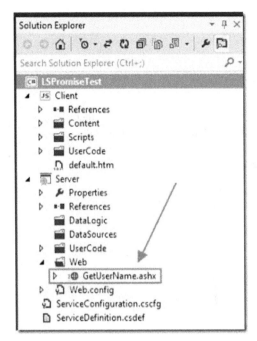

We add a **Generic File Handler** page called **GetUserName.ashx** to the **Server** project and use
the following code:

```
using System;
using System.Collections.Generic;
using System.Linq;
using System.Web;
namespace LightSwitchApplication.Web
{
    public class GetUserName : IHttpHandler
    {
        public void ProcessRequest(HttpContext context)
        {
            using (var serverContext = ServerApplicationContext.CreateContext())
            {
                context.Response.ContentType = "text/plain";
                context.Response.Write(serverContext.Application.User.Name);
            }
        }
        public bool IsReusable
        {
            get
            {
                return false;
            }
        }
    }
}
```

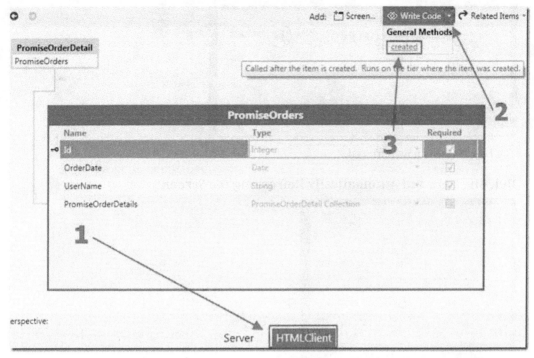

We switch back to **Logical View**, select the **HTMLClient** (tab), **Write Code**, and then the *created* method.

We add the following code:

```
myapp.PromiseOrders.created = function (entity) {
    // Set the default date for the Order
    entity.OrderDate = new Date();
    // Using a Promise object we can call the CallGetUserName function
    msls.promiseOperation(CallGetUserName).then(function PromiseSuccess(PromiseResult) {
        // Set the result of the CallGetUserName function to the
        // UserName of the entity
        entity.UserName = PromiseResult;
    });
};
// This function will be wrapped in a Promise object
function CallGetUserName(operation) {
    $.ajax({
        type: 'post',
        data: {},
        url: '../web/GetUserName.ashx',
        success: operation.code(function AjaxSuccess(AjaxResult) {
            operation.complete(AjaxResult);
        })
    });
}
```

We run the project:

The **UserName** is now retrieved.

Deleting Data and Automatically Refreshing the Screen

For the next example, we desire the ability to **delete** all the **sales records** for a single **sales person**. After the records are deleted, we want to automatically switch back to the main page.

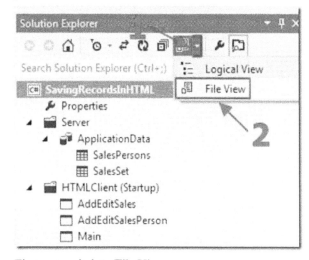

First, we switch to **File View**.

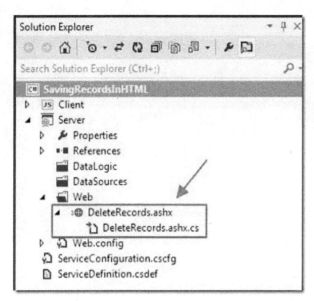

We then add a **Generic File Handler** page called **DeleteRecords.ashx** to the **Server** project and use the following code that when called by the client-side code, will delete the records:

```csharp
using System;
using System.Collections.Generic;
using System.Linq;
using System.Web;
namespace LightSwitchApplication.Web
{
    public class DeleteRecords : IHttpHandler
    {
        public void ProcessRequest(HttpContext context)
        {
            // Get the LightSwitch serverContext
            using (var serverContext = ServerApplicationContext.CreateContext())
            {
                // Minimal security is to check for IsAuthenticated
                if (serverContext.Application.User.IsAuthenticated)
                {
                    if (context.Request.QueryString["SalesPersonId"] != null)
                    {
                        // The Salesperson was passed as a parameter
                        // Note that better security would be to check if the current user
                        // should have the ability to delete the records
                        // 'serverContext.Application.User.Name' returns the current user
                        int intSalesPersonId = Convert.ToInt32(context.Request.QueryString["SalesPersonId"]);
                        // Get the Sales records to delete
                        var result = from Sales in serverContext.DataWorkspace.ApplicationData
                                        .SalesSet.GetQuery().Execute()
                                     where Sales.SalesPerson.Id == intSalesPersonId
                                     select Sales;
                        // Loop through each record found
                        foreach (var item in result)
                        {
                            // Delete the record
                            item.Delete();
                            // Save changes
                            serverContext.DataWorkspace.ApplicationData.SaveChanges();
                        }
                        // Return a response
                        // We could return any potential errors
                        context.Response.ContentType = "text/plain";
                        context.Response.Write("complete");
                    }
                }
            }
        }
        public bool IsReusable
        {
            get
            {
                return false;
            }
        }
    }
}
```

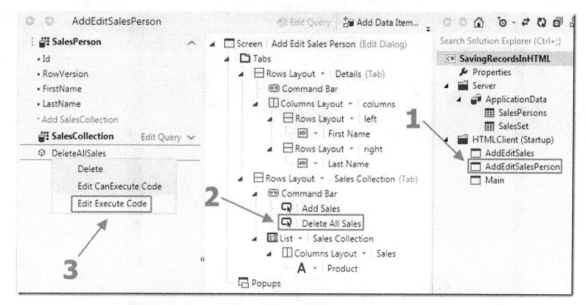

We switch back to **Logical View**, open the **AddEditSalesPerson** screen, add a **button**, and then select **Edit Execute Code** for the **button**.

We use the following code that will call the **Generic File Handler (DeleteRecords.ashx)** that we created:

```
myapp.AddEditSalesPerson.DeleteAllSales_execute = function (screen) {
    // Get selected SalesPersonId
    var SalesPersonId = screen.SalesPerson.Id;
    $.ajax({
        type: 'post',
        data: {},
        url: '../web/DeleteRecords.ashx?SalesPersonId=' + SalesPersonId,
        success: function success(result) {
            // Navigate back to main page
            myapp.navigateBack();
        }
    });
};
```

When we run the application, we can add **Sales** for a **Sales Person**, and then simply click the **Delete All Sales** button.

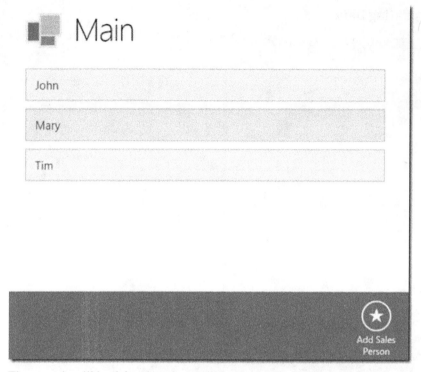

The records will be deleted, and we will be automatically navigated back to the main page.

Inserting and Updating Data

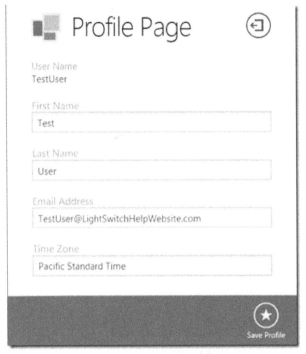

We will now look at an example that inserts and updates data using **Server Application Context**.

The Sample Application

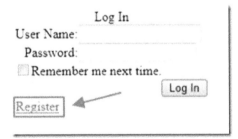

This sample application starts with a **Login** screen we created. Normally, you don't need to do this because a popup login box will automatically appear when you have authentication enabled, and a call is made to a collection that requires authentication. In this example, we will retrieve and save data manually so we have to make a **Login** page.

If we click the **Register** button, it takes us to a page that allows us to create an account.

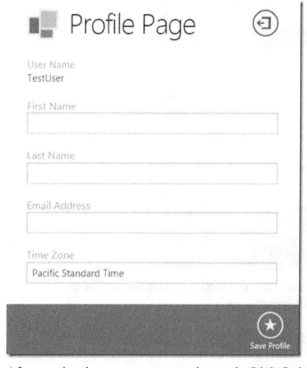

After creating the account, we are taken to the **LightSwitch** application and automatically logged in. The **User Name** displays at the top, and a default **Time Zone** is set. As will be demonstrated later, this data is generated server-side using custom code that we have full control over.

What makes this different from the normal LightSwitch screen is:

- If the user does not have a **Profile**, default data is displayed.

- If the user does have a **Profile**, their saved **Profile** is displayed.

There is only a **Save Profile** button to create and save the **Profile,** not a separate *Add Profile* button, which we would then have to add code to disable or hide if the user has already created a **Profile**.

Even though we have taken manual control of the application, we still have access to all validation and actions in the **LightSwitch** *save pipeline*.

After the user performs an action, we have the ability to implement any resulting functionality.

Creating the Application

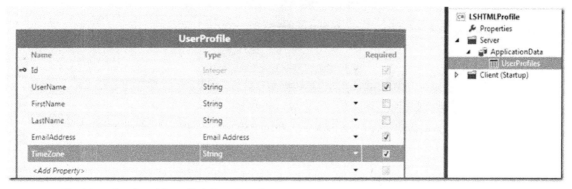

We start off with a simple table called **UserProfile**.

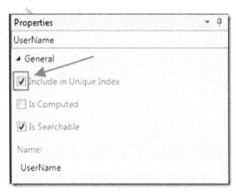

In the properties for the **UserName** field, we check the box next to **Include in Unique Index**, so the application will not allow a user to have more than one **Profile** record.

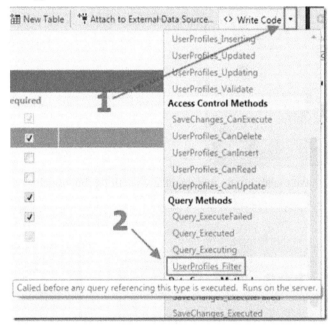

We set the **UserProfiles_Filter** by using the following code:

```
partial void UserProfiles_Filter(ref Expression<Func<UserProfile, bool>> filter)
{
    // Apply filter if user does not have SecurityAdministration Permission
    if (!this.Application.User.HasPermission(Permissions.SecurityAdministration))
    {
        // User can only see and edit their own Profile
        filter = x => x.UserName == this.Application.User.Name;
    }
}
```

This limits a user's access to his own **Profile**.

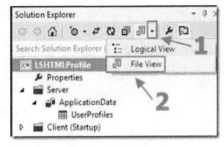

Next, we switch to **File View**.

If a **Login** page already exists, we delete it and add a **Login** page using the following code:

```
<%@ Page Language="C#" AutoEventWireup="true"
    CodeBehind="Login.aspx.cs"
    Inherits="LightSwitchApplication.Login" %>
<!DOCTYPE html>
<html xmlns="http://www.w3.org/1999/xhtml">
<head runat="server">
    <title>Login Page</title>
</head>
<body>
    <form id="form1" runat="server">
    <div>
        <asp:Login ID="LoginControl" runat="server"
            CreateUserText="Register"
            CreateUserUrl="~/Web/Default.aspx"
            DestinationPageUrl="~/HTMLClient/Default.htm">
        </asp:Login>
    </div>
    </form>
</body>
</html>
```

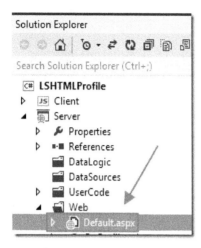

We add a **Registration** page using the following code:

```
<%@ Page Language="C#" AutoEventWireup="true"
    CodeBehind="Default.aspx.cs"
    Inherits="LightSwitchApplication.Web.Default" %>
<!DOCTYPE html>
<html xmlns="http://www.w3.org/1999/xhtml">
<head runat="server">
    <title>Create New User</title>
</head>
<body>
    <form id="form1" runat="server">
    <div>
    <asp:CreateUserWizard ID="CreateUserWizard1" runat="server"
        FinishDestinationPageUrl="../../HTMLClient/default.htm">
        <WizardSteps>
            <asp:CreateUserWizardStep ID="CreateUserWizardStep1" runat="server" />
            <asp:CompleteWizardStep ID="CompleteWizardStep1" runat="server">
                <ContentTemplate>
                    <table>
                        <tr>
                            <td align="center" colspan="2">Complete</td>
                        </tr>
                        <tr>
                            <td>Your account has been successfully created.</td>
                        </tr>
                        <tr>
                            <td align="right" colspan="2" style="text-align: center">
                                [<a href="../HTMLClient/default.htm">continue</a>]</td>
                        </tr>
                    </table>
                </ContentTemplate>
            </asp:CompleteWizardStep>
        </WizardSteps>
    </asp:CreateUserWizard>
    </div>
    </form>
</body>
</html>
```

Implementing Generic File Handlers (.ashx)

We will now load and save the data manually, rather than by using the built-in **LightSwitch** code.

We create a **Generic File Handler** called **GetProfile.ashx** to get the **Profile** data for the currently logged in user, using the following code:

```csharp
using System;
using System.Collections.Generic;
using System.Linq;
using System.Web;
namespace LightSwitchApplication.Web
{
    [Serializable]
    public class userProfile
    {
        public string UserName { get; set; }
        public string FirstName { get; set; }
        public string LastName { get; set; }
        public string EmailAddress { get; set; }
        public string TimeZone { get; set; }
        public string LightBulbStatus { get; set; }
    }
    public class GetProfile : IHttpHandler
    {
        public void ProcessRequest(HttpContext context)
        {
            using (var serverContext = ServerApplicationContext.CreateContext())
            {
                // Get the current user
                string strCurrentUserName = serverContext.Application.User.Name;
                // Instantiate userProfile class
                userProfile objUserProfile = new userProfile();
                // Try to get the Profile
                objUserProfile = (from User_Profile in serverContext.DataWorkspace.ApplicationData
                                        .UserProfiles.GetQuery().Execute()
                                  where User_Profile.UserName == strCurrentUserName
                                  select new userProfile
                                  {
                                      UserName = User_Profile.UserName,
                                      FirstName = User_Profile.FirstName,
                                      LastName = User_Profile.LastName,
                                      EmailAddress = User_Profile.EmailAddress,
                                      TimeZone = User_Profile.TimeZone
                                  }).FirstOrDefault();
                if (objUserProfile == null) // No Profile found
                {
                    // Create a Default Profile
                    objUserProfile = new userProfile();
                    objUserProfile.UserName = strCurrentUserName;
                    objUserProfile.FirstName = "";
                    objUserProfile.LastName = "";
                    objUserProfile.EmailAddress = "";
                    objUserProfile.TimeZone = TimeZoneInfo.Local.StandardName;
                    objUserProfile.LightBulbStatus = "Off";
                }
                // Create JavaScriptSerializer
                System.Web.Script.Serialization.JavaScriptSerializer jsonSerializer =
                    new System.Web.Script.Serialization.JavaScriptSerializer();
                // Output as JSON
                context.Response.Write(jsonSerializer.Serialize(objUserProfile));
            }
        }
        public bool IsReusable
        {
            get
            {
                return false;
            }
        }
    }
}
```

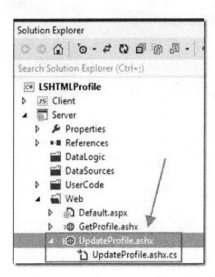

Next, we create a **Generic File Handler** called **UpdateProfile.ashx** to save the data using the following code:

```csharp
using System;
using System.Collections.Generic;
using System.Linq;
using System.Text;
using System.Web;
using System.Configuration;
using System.Net;
using System.Web.Security;
namespace LightSwitchApplication.Web
{
    public class UpdateProfile : IHttpHandler
    {
        public void ProcessRequest(HttpContext context)
        {
            string strResponse = "";
            // Get the LightSwitch serverContext
            using (var serverContext = ServerApplicationContext.CreateContext())
            {
                // Minimal security is to check for IsAuthenticated
                if (serverContext.Application.User.IsAuthenticated)
                {
                    string strFirstName = Convert.ToString(context.Request.Params["FirstName"]);
                    string strLastName = Convert.ToString(context.Request.Params["LastName"]);
                    string strEmailAddress = Convert.ToString(context.Request.Params["EmailAddress"]);
                    string strTimeZone = Convert.ToString(context.Request.Params["TimeZone"]);
                    string strLightBulbStatus = Convert.ToString(context.Request.Params["LightBulbStatus"]);
                    // Get the current user
                    string strCurrentUserName = serverContext.Application.User.Name;
                    var objUserProfile = (from User_Profile in serverContext.DataWorkspace.ApplicationData
                                            .UserProfiles.GetQuery().Execute()
                                          where User_Profile.UserName == strCurrentUserName
                                          select User_Profile).FirstOrDefault();
                    if (objUserProfile != null) // Update existing Profile
                    {
                        try
                        {
                            objUserProfile.FirstName = strFirstName;
                            objUserProfile.LastName = strLastName;
                            objUserProfile.EmailAddress = strEmailAddress;
                            objUserProfile.TimeZone = strTimeZone;
                            serverContext.DataWorkspace.ApplicationData.SaveChanges();
                        }
                        catch (Exception ex)
                        {
                            strResponse = ShowError(ex);
                        }
                    }
                    else // Add new Profile
                    {
                        try
                        {
                            var newProfile =
                                serverContext.DataWorkspace.ApplicationData.UserProfiles.AddNew();
                            newProfile.UserName = strCurrentUserName;
                            newProfile.FirstName = strFirstName;
                            newProfile.LastName = strLastName;
                            newProfile.EmailAddress = strEmailAddress;
                            newProfile.TimeZone = strTimeZone;
                            serverContext.DataWorkspace.ApplicationData.SaveChanges();
                        }
                        catch (Exception ex)
                        {
                            strResponse = ShowError(ex);
                        }
                    }
                }
            }
            // Return a response
            context.Response.ContentType = "text/plain";
            context.Response.Write(strResponse);
        }
```

```csharp
// Utility
#region ShowError
private string ShowError(Exception ex)
{
    string strError = "";
    Microsoft.LightSwitch.ValidationException ValidationErrors =
        ex as Microsoft.LightSwitch.ValidationException;
    if (ValidationErrors != null)
    {
        StringBuilder sbErrorMessage = new StringBuilder();
        foreach (var error in ValidationErrors.ValidationResults)
        {
            sbErrorMessage.Append(string.Format(" {0} ", error.Message));
        }
        strError = sbErrorMessage.ToString();
    }
    else
    {
        // This is a simple error -- just show Message
        strError = ex.Message;
    }
    return strError;
}
#endregion
#region IsReusable
public bool IsReusable
{
    get
    {
        return false;
    }
}
#endregion
    }
}
```

Create the LightSwitch Page

Now, we switch back to **Logical View** and add a new **Screen.** We do not select any data for it.

When the **Screen** opens in the **Screen** designer, we select **Add Data Item**…

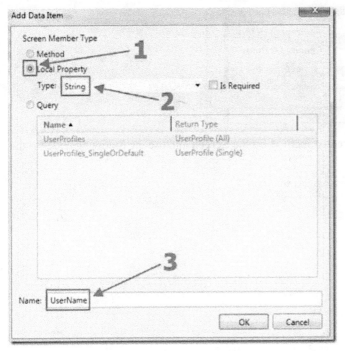

We add a **Property** for each data field that we need.

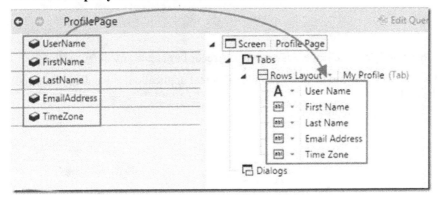

The **Properties** will show up in the *View Model* on the *left-hand* side of the **Screen** designer. We now drag and drop them onto the layout to bind **Controls** to them.

Loading the Data

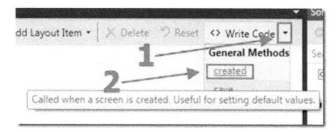

To load the data, we select the **created** method for the **Screen** and use the following code for the method:

```
myapp.ProfilePage.created = function (screen) {
    // Call GetProfileUpdateProfile.ashx .ashx
    // to get the Users Profile
    $.ajax({
        type: 'post',
        data: {},
        url: '../web/GetProfile.ashx',
        success: function success(result) {
            // Parse the JSON returned
            var objProfile = jQuery.parseJSON(result);
            // Fill in the values on the Screen
            screen.UserName = objProfile.UserName;
            screen.FirstName = objProfile.FirstName;
            screen.LastName = objProfile.LastName;
            screen.EmailAddress = objProfile.EmailAddress;
            screen.TimeZone = objProfile.TimeZone;
        }
    });
};
```

Notice the code does not determine if there is an existing record or create any default values.

All the business logic, logic that can be quite complex in a real application, is handled in normal ASP.NET code behind.

Saving the Data

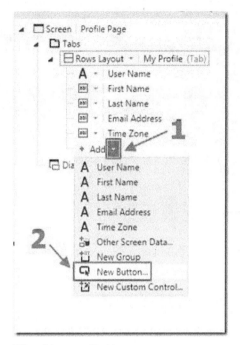

We add a new **Button**.

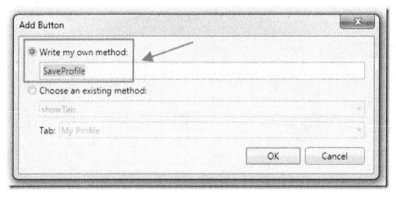

We call it **SaveProfile**.

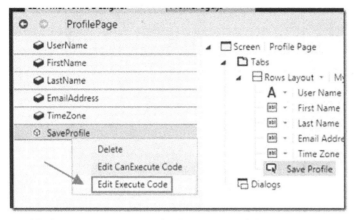

It will show up as a **Method** in the *View Model*.

We *right-click* on it and select **Edit Execute Code**, and use the following code for the method:

```
myapp.ProfilePage.SaveProfile_execute = function (screen) {
    // Get values from the Screen
    var paramFirstName = screen.FirstName;
    var paramLastName = screen.LastName;
    var paramEmailAddress = screen.EmailAddress;
    var paramTimeZone = screen.TimeZone;
    // Call UpdateProfile.ashx
    // to update values in database
    $.ajax({
        type: 'post',
        data: {
            FirstName: paramFirstName,
            LastName: paramLastName,
            EmailAddress: paramEmailAddress,
            TimeZone: paramTimeZone,
        },
        url: '../web/UpdateProfile.ashx',
        success: function success(result) {
            // Show result
            if (result != "") {
                alert(result);
            }
            else {
                alert("Saved");
            }
        }
    });
};
```

Again, note we simply call the handler and display any errors. The amount of **JavaScript** we are required to write is minimal.

Creating ASP.NET Web Forms CRUD Pages Using ServerApplicationContext

In our final example of **ServerApplicationContext**, we will use an **ASP.NET Web Form** page.

The Application

		Description	Person Calling	Phone Number	Call Type
Delete	Update	Customer Called	John Doe	2135551212	Service ▼
Delete	Update	Vendor Called	Tim Smith	7145551212	Other ▼
Delete	Update	Repair requested	Sandy Jones	8185551212	Service ▼

Insert New:

Description	Quote requested
Person Calling	Kim Harris
Phone Number	3105551212|
Call Type	Sales ▼

Submit

The sample application allows you to **create** new call center records in the form at the bottom, and **display** them in the grid at the top. You can **update** and **delete** the items in the grid.

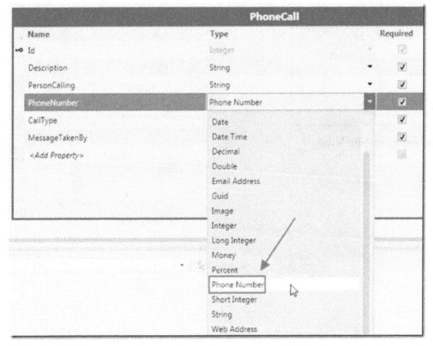

LightSwitch has many features that allow you to easily implement business rules, security rules, and business types. In this example, the *Phone Number* business type is set for the **PhoneNumber** field in the **PhoneCall** table.

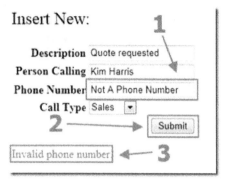

Without the need to write a single line of code, the business type is enforced.

Creating the Web Page

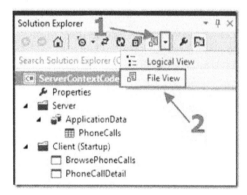

The first step is to switch to **File View**.

Next, we select **Add** then **New Item...** in the **Web** folder of the **Server** project.

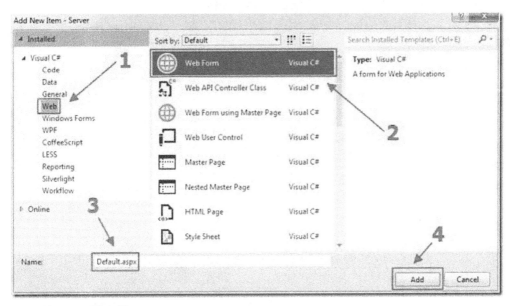

We add a new **Web Form** page.

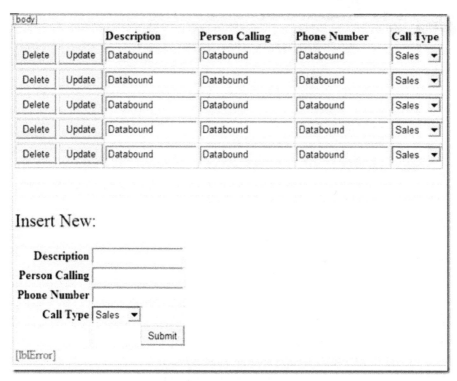

		Description	Person Calling	Phone Number	Call Type
Delete	Update	Databound	Databound	Databound	Sales ▼
Delete	Update	Databound	Databound	Databound	Sales ▼
Delete	Update	Databound	Databound	Databound	Sales ▼
Delete	Update	Databound	Databound	Databound	Sales ▼
Delete	Update	Databound	Databound	Databound	Sales ▼

Insert New:

Description	
Person Calling	
Phone Number	
Call Type	Sales ▼
	Submit

[lblError]

We use the following code in the **Default.aspx** file:

```
<%@ Page Language="C#" AutoEventWireup="true" CodeBehind="Default.aspx.cs" Inherits="LightSwitchApplication.Web.Default" %>
<!DOCTYPE html>
<html xmlns="http://www.w3.org/1999/xhtml">
<head id="Head1" runat="server">
    <title>Phone Calls</title>
</head>
<body>
    <form id="form1" runat="server">
        <div>
            <style type="text/css">
                .style1
                {
                    font-weight: normal;
                }
            </style>
            <asp:DataList ID="dlPhoneCalls" runat="server" GridLines="Both">
                <HeaderTemplate>
                     </td><td>
                        <strong>Description</strong> </td>
                    <td>
                        <strong>Person Calling</strong>
                    </td>
                    <td>
                        <strong>Phone Number</strong>
                    </td>
                    <td>
                        <strong>Call Type</strong>
                </HeaderTemplate>
                <ItemTemplate>
                    <asp:Button ID="btnDelete" runat="server" Text="Delete"
                        CommandArgument='<%# Eval("Id") %>' OnClick="btnDelete_Click" />
                    <asp:Button ID="btnUpdate" runat="server" OnClick="btnUpdate_Click"
                        Text="Update" CommandArgument='<%# Eval("Id") %>' />
                    </td><td>
                        <asp:TextBox ID="Description" runat="server" Text='<%# Eval("Description") %>' />
                    </td>
                    <td>
                        <asp:TextBox ID="PersonCalling" runat="server" Text='<%# Eval("PersonCalling") %>' />
                    </td>
                    <td>
                        <asp:TextBox ID="PhoneNumber" runat="server" Text='<%# Eval("PhoneNumber") %>' />
                    </td>
                    <td>
                        <asp:Label ID="lblCallType" runat="server" Text='<%# Eval("CallType") %>' Visible="False" />
                        <asp:DropDownList ID="ddlGridCallType" runat="server"
                            OnDataBound="ddlCallType_DataBound">
                            <asp:ListItem>Sales</asp:ListItem>
                            <asp:ListItem>Service</asp:ListItem>
                            <asp:ListItem>Other</asp:ListItem>
                        </asp:DropDownList>
                </ItemTemplate>
            </asp:DataList>
```

```html
<p>
     
</p>
<h2 class="style1">Insert New:</h2>
<table>
    <tr>
        <td align="right">
            <strong>Description</strong>
        </td>
        <td>
            <asp:TextBox ID="txtDescription" runat="server"></asp:TextBox>
        </td>
    </tr>
    <tr>
        <td align="right">
            <strong>Person Calling</strong>
        </td>
        <td>
            <asp:TextBox ID="txtPersonCalling" runat="server"></asp:TextBox>
        </td>
    </tr>
    <tr>
        <td align="right">
            <strong>Phone Number</strong>
        </td>
        <td>
            <asp:TextBox ID="txtPhoneNumber" runat="server"></asp:TextBox>
        </td>
    </tr>
    <tr>
        <td align="right">
            <strong>Call Type</strong>
        </td>
        <td>
            <asp:DropDownList ID="ddlCallType" runat="server">
                <asp:ListItem>Sales</asp:ListItem>
                <asp:ListItem>Service</asp:ListItem>
                <asp:ListItem>Other</asp:ListItem>
            </asp:DropDownList>
        </td>
    </tr>
    <tr>
        <td align="right"> 
        </td>
        <td align="right">
            <asp:Button ID="btnSubmit" runat="server" OnClick="btnSubmit_Click" Text="Submit" />
        </td>
    </tr>
</table>
<asp:Label ID="lblError" runat="server" EnableViewState="False" ForeColor="Red"></asp:Label>
</div>
</form>
</body>
</html>
```

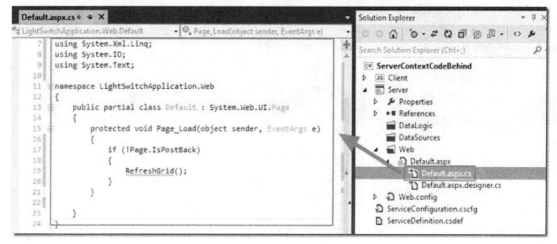

Next, we use the following code in the **Default.aspx.cs** file:

```
using System.Xml.Linq;
using System.IO;
using System.Text;
namespace LightSwitchApplication.Web
{
    public partial class Default : System.Web.UI.Page
    {
        protected void Page_Load(object sender, EventArgs e)
        {
            if (!Page.IsPostBack)
            {
                RefreshGrid();
            }
        }
    }
}
```

Server Context

The **server context** is automatically cached in the *Current* property; we use the following code
to only create it when needed:

```
#region GetServerContext
private static ServerApplicationContext GetServerContext()
{
    ServerApplicationContext serverContext =
        (LightSwitchApplication.ServerApplicationContext)ServerApplicationContext.Current;
    if (serverContext == null)
    {
        serverContext =
            (LightSwitchApplication.ServerApplicationContext)ServerApplicationContext.CreateContext();
    }
    return serverContext;
}
#endregion
```

Display Data

To display data, we use the following method:

```
private void RefreshGrid()
{
    // Get all PhoneCalls
    using (var serverContext = GetServerContext())
    {
        var result = from PhoneCalls in serverContext.DataWorkspace.ApplicationData
                        .PhoneCalls.GetQuery().Execute()
                    select PhoneCalls;
        dlPhoneCalls.DataSource = result;
        dlPhoneCalls.DataBind();
    }
}
```

Also, to set the dropdown in each row to the proper value, we use the following code:

```
protected void ddlCallType_DataBound(object sender, EventArgs e)
{
    // Get an instance of the DropDownList
    DropDownList objDropDownList = (DropDownList)sender;
    // Get the selected value from the hidden Label
    Label objLabel = (Label)objDropDownList.Parent.FindControl("lblCallType");
    // Set the selected value in the DropDownList
    objDropDownList.SelectedValue = objLabel.Text;
}
```

Insert Data

To insert data, we use the following code:

```
protected void btnSubmit_Click(object sender, EventArgs e)
{
    using (var serverContext = GetServerContext())
    {
        try
        {
            // Create a new PhoneCall
            var objPhoneCall = serverContext.DataWorkspace.ApplicationData.PhoneCalls.AddNew();
            // Set values
            objPhoneCall.CallType = ddlCallType.SelectedValue;
            objPhoneCall.Description = txtDescription.Text;
            objPhoneCall.PersonCalling = txtPersonCalling.Text;
            objPhoneCall.PhoneNumber = txtPhoneNumber.Text;
            objPhoneCall.MessageTakenBy =
                (this.User.Identity.Name != "") ? this.User.Identity.Name : "[unknown]";
            // Save changes
            serverContext.DataWorkspace.ApplicationData.SaveChanges();
            // Refresh the Grid
            RefreshGrid();
        }
        catch (Exception ex)
        {
            ShowError(ex);
            return;
        }
    }
}
```

Update Data

To update data, we use the following code:

```csharp
protected void btnUpdate_Click(object sender, EventArgs e)
{
    // Get an instance of the Button
    Button UpdateButton = (Button)sender;
    // Get the ID of the current record from the CommandArgument
    int intID = Convert.ToInt32(UpdateButton.CommandArgument);
    using (var serverContext = GetServerContext())
    {
        try
        {
            // Get the record
            var result = (from PhoneCalls in serverContext.DataWorkspace.ApplicationData
                            .PhoneCalls.GetQuery().Execute()
                            where PhoneCalls.Id == intID
                            select PhoneCalls).FirstOrDefault();
            if (result != null)
            {
                // Get the values
                TextBox Description =
                    (TextBox)UpdateButton.Parent.FindControl("Description");
                TextBox PersonCalling =
                    (TextBox)UpdateButton.Parent.FindControl("PersonCalling");
                TextBox PhoneNumber =
                    (TextBox)UpdateButton.Parent.FindControl("PhoneNumber");
                DropDownList ddlGridCallType =
                    (DropDownList)UpdateButton.Parent.FindControl("ddlGridCallType");
                // Update the record
                result.Description = Description.Text;
                result.PersonCalling = PersonCalling.Text;
                result.PhoneNumber = PhoneNumber.Text;
                result.CallType = ddlGridCallType.SelectedValue;
                // Save changes
                serverContext.DataWorkspace.ApplicationData.SaveChanges();
                // Refresh the Grid
                RefreshGrid();
            }
        }
        catch (Exception ex)
        {
            ShowError(ex);
            return;
        }
    }
}
```

Delete Data

To delete data, we use the following method:

```csharp
protected void btnDelete_Click(object sender, EventArgs e)
{
    // Get an instance of the Button
    Button DeleteButton = (Button)sender;
    // Get the ID of the current record from the CommandArgument
    int intID = Convert.ToInt32(DeleteButton.CommandArgument);
    using (var serverContext = GetServerContext())
    {
        try
        {
            // Get the record
            var result = (from PhoneCalls in serverContext.DataWorkspace.ApplicationData
                          .PhoneCalls.GetQuery().Execute()
                          where PhoneCalls.Id == intID
                          select PhoneCalls).FirstOrDefault();
            if (result != null)
            {
                // Delete the record
                result.Delete();
                // Save changes
                serverContext.DataWorkspace.ApplicationData.SaveChanges();
                // Refresh the Grid
                RefreshGrid();
            }
        }
        catch (Exception ex)
        {
            ShowError(ex);
            return;
        }
    }
}
```

Validation Errors

To show validation errors, we use the following method:

```csharp
private void ShowError(Exception ex)
{
    string strError = "";
    Microsoft.LightSwitch.ValidationException ValidationErrors = ex as Microsoft.LightSwitch.ValidationException;
    if (ValidationErrors != null)
    {
        StringBuilder sbErrorMessage = new StringBuilder();
        foreach (var error in ValidationErrors.ValidationResults)
        {
            sbErrorMessage.Append(string.Format("<p>{0}</p>", error.Message));
        }
        strError = sbErrorMessage.ToString();
    }
    else
    {
        // This is a simple error -- just show Message
        strError = ex.Message;
    }
    lblError.Text = strError;
}
```

Display the Web Page

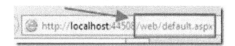

When we run the application, we have to navigate to */web/Default.aspx* to see the page.

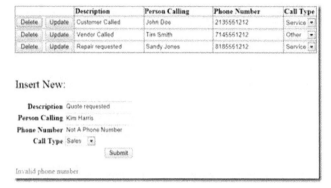

The application will allow us to create, read, update, and delete data.

Using WCF RIA Services

The sample code for this section can be obtained at the link "Creating a WCF RIA Service for Visual Studio 2012 (Update 2 and higher)" at http://lightswitchhelpwebsite.com/Downloads.aspx.

The primary reasons you may need to use **WCF RIA Services** with **Visual Studio LightSwitch** are to:

- Combine more than one entity into a single entity.
- Eliminate unneeded columns in an entity to improve performance, otherwise large amounts of data, for example pictures, will be transmitted even when they are not shown.
- Implement calculated fields that allow the resulting values to be searchable and sortable.

Also, note that the **LightSwitch OData** services return one **Entity** collection at a time. This makes grouping and totaling across **Entity** collections difficult. Using **WCF RIA Services** provides a clean elegant solution.

The Sample Application

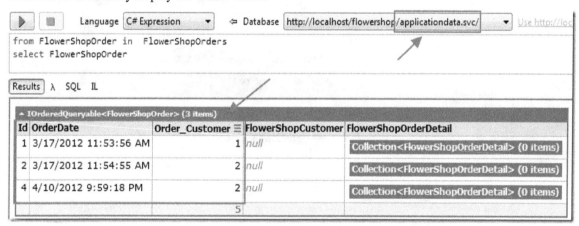

	FlowerShopOrder
Name	**Type**
Id	Integer
FlowerShopCustomer	FlowerShopCustomer
OrderDate	Date Time
FlowerShopOrderDetail	FlowerShopOrderDetail Collection
OrderTotal	Money
OrderName	String

In the **Flower Shop** application used in the tutorial, **Calling LightSwitch 2011 OData Using Server Side Code** (http://bit.ly/GCH8cT), it has computed fields in the **FlowerShopOrder** entity.

This allows us to easily display the **Order Total**.

| | Language | C# Expression ▼ | ⇐ Database | http://localhost/flowershop/applicationdata.svc/ ▼ | Use http://loc |

```
from FlowerShopOrder in  FlowerShopOrders
select FlowerShopOrder
```

Results λ SQL IL

	▲ IOrderedQueryable<FlowerShopOrder> (3 items)			
Id	**OrderDate**	**Order_Customer** ≡	**FlowerShopCustomer**	**FlowerShopOrderDetail**
1	3/17/2012 11:53:56 AM	1	null	Collection<FlowerShopOrderDetail> (0 items)
2	3/17/2012 11:54:55 AM	2	null	Collection<FlowerShopOrderDetail> (0 items)
4	4/10/2012 9:59:18 PM	2	null	Collection<FlowerShopOrderDetail> (0 items)
		5		

However, if we use a tool such as **LinqPad** (www.linqpad.net) to connect to the **OData** service for that entity, we see it does not contain the **Order Total**.

To get this data, it requires additional queries of the **Product Entity** to get the **Product** price, and all the related **Order Detail** entities to calculate the **Order Total**.

This is a problem because not only does it require additional database queries, it requires the client consuming the **OData** feed to now be responsible for complex business logic.

We can create an **OData** service with these computed fields using a **WCF RIA Service**.

Create A WCF RIA Service

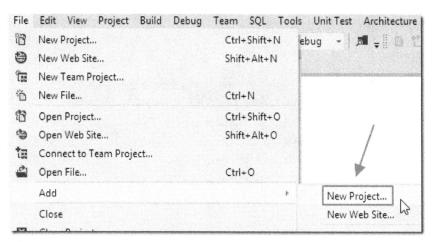

First, **Add a New Project** to the existing **LightSwitch** project.

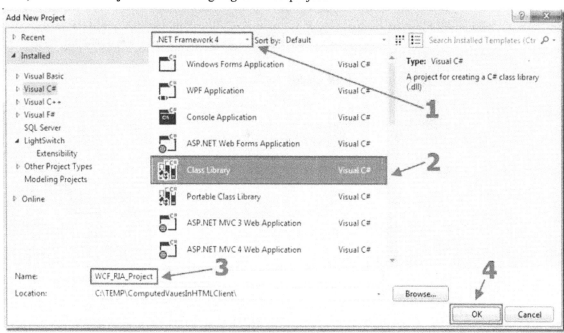

Create a **.NET Framework 4 Class Library** called **WCF_RIA_Project**.

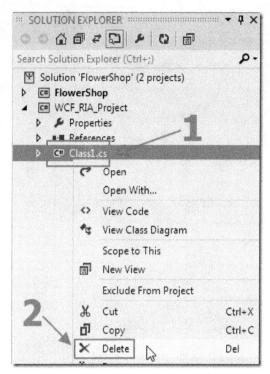

Delete the **Class1.cs** file that is automatically created.

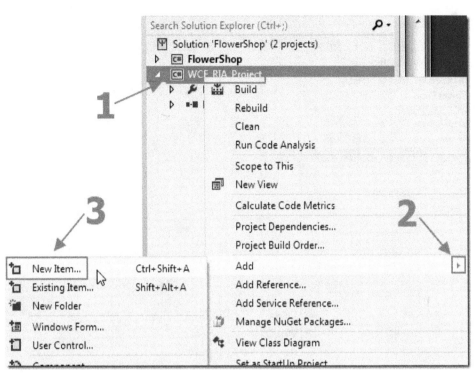

Add a **New Item** to the **WCF_RIA_Project.**

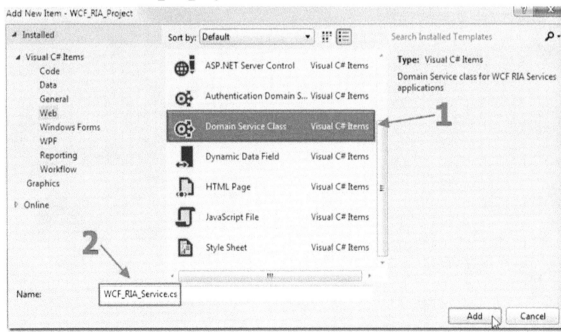

Add a **Domain Service Class** called **WCF_RIA_Service.cs.**

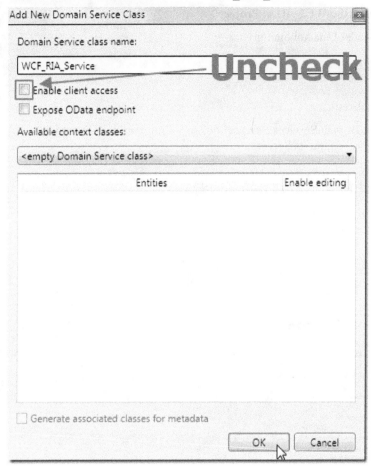

When the **Add New Domain Service Class** box comes up, *uncheck* **Enable client access.** Click **OK**.

The reason we do this is because this domain class will be exposed by **LightSwitch** and the data will pass through the **LightSwitch** security and business rules.

We need additional references.

Add the following references to the **WCF_RIA_Project**:

- System.ComponentModel.DataAnnotations
- System.Configuration
- System.Data.Entity
- System.Runtime.Serialization
- System.ServiceModel.DomainServices.Server (Look in %ProgramFiles%\Microsoft SDKs\RIA Services\v1.0\Libraries\Server)
- System.Web

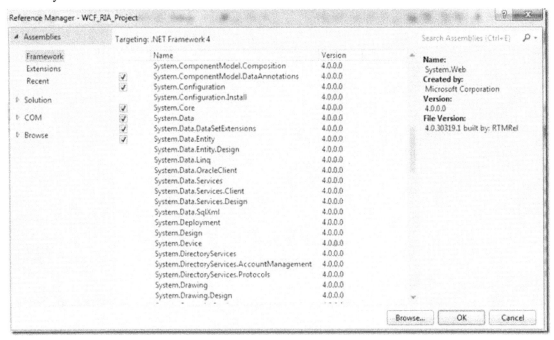

Add the following *Using Statements* to the class:

- using System.Data.EntityClient;
- using System.Web.Configuration;
- using LightSwitchApplication.Implementation;

LightSwitchApplication will display with a squiggly red line because the class is missing, but it will be added in the next step.

```
namespace WCF_RIA_Project
{
    using System;
    using System.Collections.Generic;
    using System.ComponentModel;
    using System.ComponentModel.DataAnnotations;
    using System.Linq;
    using System.ServiceModel.DomainServices.Hosting;
    using System.ServiceModel.DomainServices.Server;
    using System.Data.EntityClient;
    using System.Web.Configuration;
    using LightSwitchApplication.Implementation;


    // TODO: Create methods containing your application logic.
    // TODO: add the EnableClientAccessAttribute to this class t
```

Reference the LightSwitch Object Context

Now, we will add code from the **LightSwitch** project to our **WCF RIA Service** project. We will add a class that **LightSwitch** automatically creates, which connects to the database **LightSwitch** uses.

We will use this class in our **WCF RIA Service** to communicate with the **LightSwitch** database.

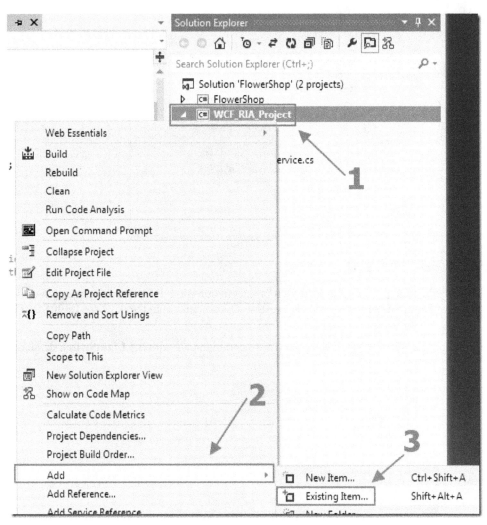

Next, we *right-click* on the **WCF_RIA_Project**. Then we select **Add** and **Existing Item**.

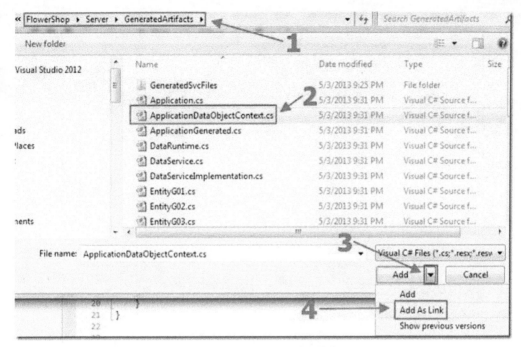

Now we navigate to **Server\GeneratedArtifacts** (in the **LightSwitch** project) and click on **ApplicationDataObjectContext.cs** and **Add As Link**.

We used *Add As Link* so that whenever **LightSwitch** updates this class, our **WCF RIA Service** is also updated. This is how our **WCF RIA Service** is able to see any new **Entities** (tables) that are added, deleted, or changed.

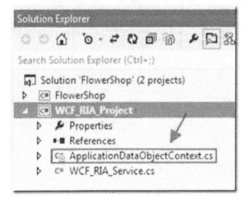

The file will show in the project.

Create the Domain Service

Replace the entire code for the **WCF_RIA_Service.cs** file with the following:

```csharp
namespace WCF_RIA_Project
{
    using System;
    using System.Collections.Generic;
    using System.ComponentModel;
    using System.ComponentModel.DataAnnotations;
    using System.Linq;
    using System.ServiceModel.DomainServices.Hosting;
    using System.ServiceModel.DomainServices.Server;
    using System.Data.EntityClient;
    using System.Web.Configuration;
    using LightSwitchApplication.Implementation;
    // This class is used as the class that is returned
    // This can have any 'shape' you desire
    // Make sure this is outside of the WCF_RIA_Service class
    // but inside the WCF_RIA_Project namespace
    public class EnhancedFlowerShopOrder
    {
        [Key]
        public int ID { get; set; }
        public DateTime OrderDate { get; set; }
        public string FirstName { get; set; }
        public string LastName { get; set; }
        public decimal OrderTotal { get; set; }
    }
    public class WCF_RIA_Service : DomainService
    {
        // This Context property is code that connects to the LightSwitch database
        // The code in the Database connection region can be reused as it is
        #region Database connection
        private ApplicationData m_context;
        public ApplicationData Context
        {
            get
            {
                if (this.m_context == null)
                {
                    string connString =
                        System.Web.Configuration.WebConfigurationManager
                        .ConnectionStrings["_IntrinsicData"].ConnectionString;
                    EntityConnectionStringBuilder builder = new EntityConnectionStringBuilder();
                    builder.Metadata =
                        "res://*/ApplicationData.csdl|res://*/ApplicationData.ssdl|res://*/ApplicationData.msl";
                    builder.Provider =
                        "System.Data.SqlClient";
                    builder.ProviderConnectionString = connString;
                    this.m_context = new ApplicationData(builder.ConnectionString);
                }
                return this.m_context;
            }
        }
        #endregion
```

```
[Query(IsDefault = true)]
public IQueryable<EnhancedFlowerShopOrder> GetAllOrders()
{
    // Get all the Orders
    var colFlowerShopOrders = from Order in this.Context.FlowerShopOrders
                              // Shape the results into the
                              // EnhancedFlowerShopOrder class
                              select new EnhancedFlowerShopOrder
                              {
                                  // The Order ID
                                  ID = Order.Id,
                                  // The Order Date
                                  OrderDate = Order.OrderDate,
                                  // The first name of the Customer
                                  FirstName = Order.FlowerShopCustomer.FirstName,
                                  // The last name of the Customer
                                  LastName = Order.FlowerShopCustomer.LastName,
                                  // The order Total
                                  OrderTotal =
                                  // Get all order details lines of the Order
                                  (from FlowerShopOrderDetail in Order.FlowerShopOrderDetail
                                   // Group the products in the Order Details
                                   group FlowerShopOrderDetail
                                   by FlowerShopOrderDetail.Id into g
                                   // Shape a new entity
                                   select new
                                   {
                                       // Create a total property that is the Quantity times the
                                       // Product price
                                       TotalOrder = g.Sum(x => x.Quantity)
                                       * g.Sum(x => x.FlowerShopProduct.Price),
                                   }).Sum(x => x.TotalOrder) // Add the sum of all the TotalOrders
                              };
    return colFlowerShopOrders;
}
// Override the Count method in order for paging to work correctly
protected override int Count<T>(IQueryable<T> query)
{
    return query.Count();
}
```

Consume the WCF RIA Service

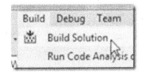

Build the solution.

You will get multiple warnings in the immediate window in Visual Studio. You can ignore them.

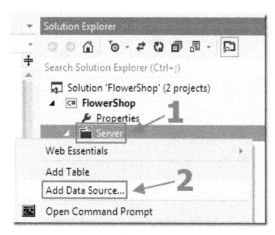

In the **Solution Explorer** (of the **LightSwitch** project), we now *right-click* on the **Server** folder and we then select **Add Data Source**.

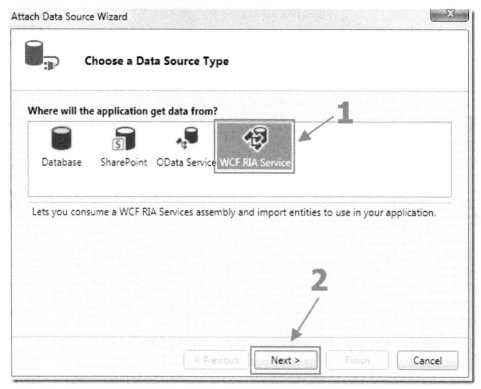

Now, select **WCF RIA Service** and click the **Next** button.

Click the **Add Reference** button.

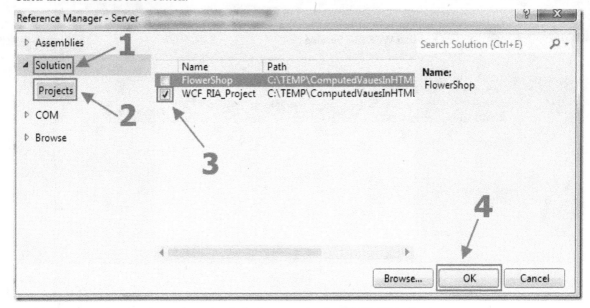

Select **Solution**, then **Projects**, then check the box next to the **WCF_RIA_Project**.

Click **OK**.

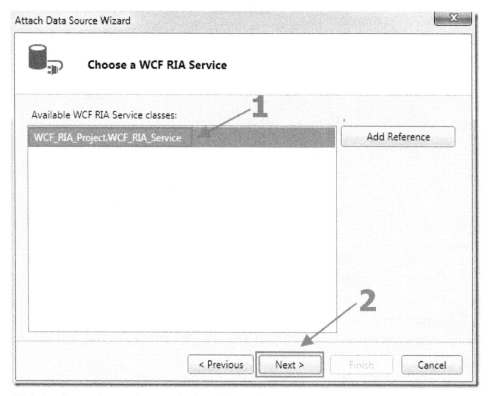

Wait for the service to show up in the selection box, select it and click **Next**.

Check the box next to the **Entities**, and click **Finish**.

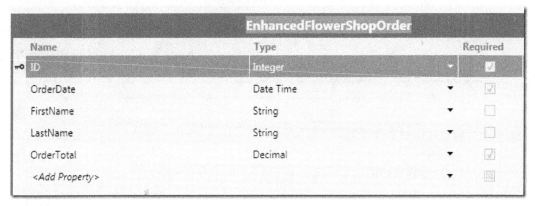

The **Entity** will display.

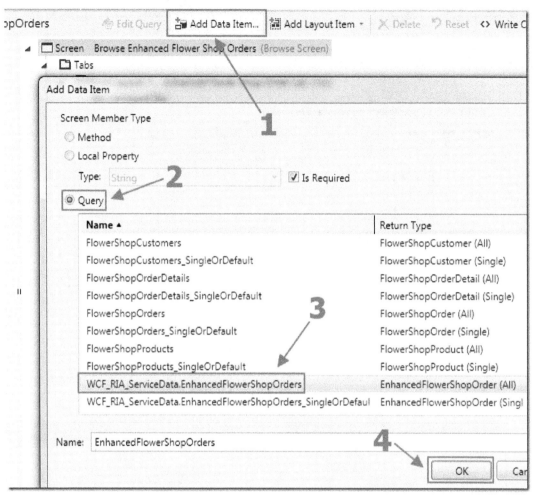

We can now add the collection to a screen as we would any other collection.

⊖ Browse Enhanced Flower Shop Orders

$483.72 3/17/2012 10:49:43 AM

$478.11 4/8/2012 7:39:25 PM

$213.11 4/10/2012 7:13:35 PM

$426.22 4/18/2012 6:18:21 AM

All the values are searchable and sortable.

Advanced JavaScript

The sample code for this section can be obtained at the links "Computed Properties with the LightSwitch HTML Client", "HUY Volume II - Visual Studio LightSwitch Advanced JavaScript Examples", and "HUY Volume III– Popups, Dirty Visual Collections, and Using Prototypes To Calculate Child Collections" at http://lightswitchhelpwebsite.com/Downloads.aspx.

Computed Properties with the LightSwitch HTML Client

The current version of the **LightSwitch HTML Client** does not expose the computed properties created at the **Entity** level. Here are a few methods you can use.

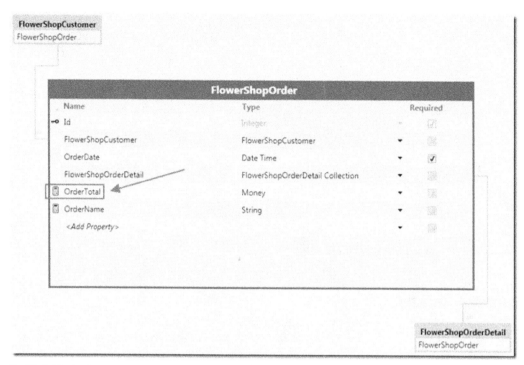

In **LightSwitch**, we can create a computed column and use the following code for the result:

```
partial void OrderTotal_Compute(ref decimal? result)
{
    decimal dOrderTotal = 0.0M;
    // Get OrderDetails that have products
    var colOrderDetails = from OrderDetails in this.FlowerShopOrderDetail
                          where OrderDetails.FlowerShopProduct != null
                          select OrderDetails;
    foreach (var order in colOrderDetails)
    {
        dOrderTotal = dOrderTotal + (order.Quantity * order.FlowerShopProduct.Price);
    }
    result = dOrderTotal;
}
```

When we consume the **Entity** in the **LightSwitch** Silverlight client...

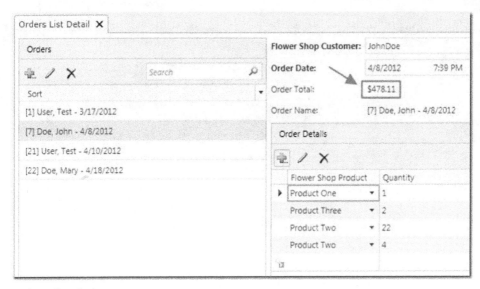

...the value shows.

However, when we create a page with the **LightSwitch HTML Client**, we don't have access to the computed property.

Using JavaScript

We can create the computed property using **JavaScript**.

First, we **Add Data Item** to the **Visual Studio LightSwitch HTML Client** screen.

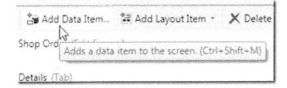

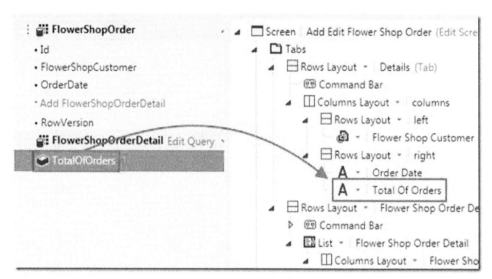

We add an **Integer** property to the screen called **TotalOfOrders**, and we drag it to the screen layout.

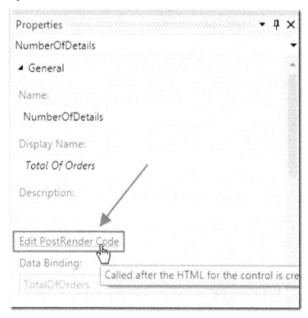

We click on the screen element, and in the **Properties**, we select **Edit PostRender Code**.

We use the following code:

```
myapp.AddEditFlowerShopOrder.NumberOfDetails_postRender = function (element, contentItem) {
    function updateTotal() {
        // Compute the total for the Order
        contentItem.screen.TotalOfOrders =
            TotalOrders(contentItem.screen.FlowerShopOrderDetail);
    }
    // Set a dataBind to update the value when the collection changes
    contentItem.dataBind("screen.FlowerShopOrderDetail.count", updateTotal)
};
// Function to compute the total for the Order
function TotalOrders(OrderDetails) {
    // Start with 0
    var TotalAmountOfOrders = 0;
    // Get the data for the collection passed
    var OrderDetail = OrderDetails.data;
    // Loop through each row
    OrderDetail.forEach(function (order) {
        // Add each row to TotalAmountOfOrders
        TotalAmountOfOrders = TotalAmountOfOrders +
            (order.Quantity * order.FlowerShopProduct.Price);
    });
    // Return TotalAmountOfOrders
    return TotalAmountOfOrders;
}
```

When we run the application, the value will now show.

Note: In this example, we only detect that the count of the records has changed. If, for example, only the price changed, you would expect the computed property to change, it would not. Also, if the list was a paged list and there were more records than the current page setting (the default is 45 records per page), it would not update properly.

However, in this example, we return the user to the main screen after making any change. When the user returns to this screen, the value is always properly updated.

Using Prototypes to Calculate Child Records

It is also possible to create computed properties using **EventListeners** to retrieve values from **JavaScript** *prototype* methods.

In this example, the **Order Detail** records attached to each **Order** have a field where you can make each one *available* or *un-available*.

In the example, on the **Edit Order** screen, the count of **available** and **un-available** *saved* **Order Detail** records for the selected **Order** are displayed.

Creating the Code

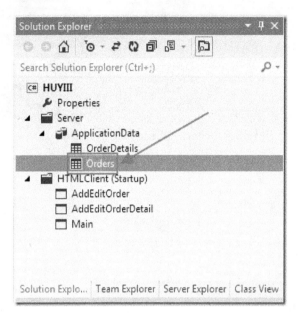

We open the **Orders** table.

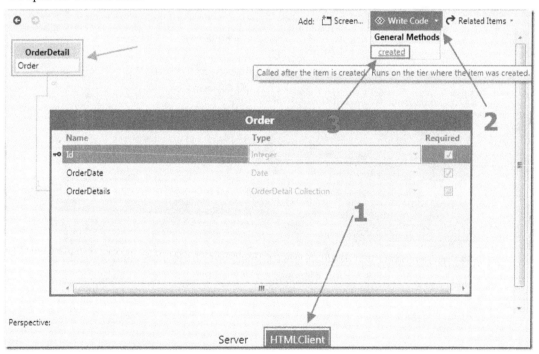

*Notice the **OrderDetail** entity is associated with the **Order** entity.*

We select the **HTMLClient** tab. Then select **Write Code** and the ***created*** method.

This allows us to create **JavaScript** code on the entity that will run no matter what screen the entity is consumed on.

We use the following code for the method:

```
myapp.Order.created = function (entity) {
    // Set Default Date
    entity.OrderDate = new Date();
};
```

We also add the following *prototype* methods outside of the *created* method:

```
// Calculated field to count Available OrderDetails
myapp.Order.prototype.getAvailable = function () {
    return this.OrderDetails.sum(function (item) {
        return item.ItemAvailable == true;
    });
};
// Calculated field to count UnAvailable OrderDetails
myapp.Order.prototype.getUnAvailable = function () {
    return this.OrderDetails.sum(function (item) {
        return item.ItemAvailable == false;
    });
};
```

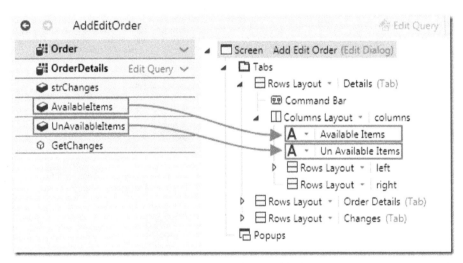

On the screen, we create two **String** properties and bind them to **label controls** on the screen.

The following code is used for the *_postRender* method for each **label control**:

```
myapp.AddEditOrder.AvailableItems_postRender = function (element, contentItem) {
    // Get the Order on the screen
    var order = contentItem.screen.Order;
    // Show the current count
    element.innerText = order.getAvailable();
    // Method that will be called on update of count
    function updateValue() {
        element.innerText = order.getAvailable();
    }
    // Add event listener
    order.OrderDetails.addEventListener(
        "collectionchange", updateValue);
    // Trigger load of OrderDetails
    order.getOrderDetails();
    // Clean up event listener
    contentItem.handleViewDispose(function () {
        parent.Children.removeEventListener(
            "collectionchange", updateValue);
    });
};
myapp.AddEditOrder.UnAvailableItems_postRender = function (element, contentItem) {
    // Get the Order on the screen
    var order = contentItem.screen.Order;
    // Show the current count
    element.innerText = order.getUnAvailable();
    // Method that will be called on update of count
    function updateValue() {
        element.innerText = order.getUnAvailable();
    }
    // Add event listener
    order.OrderDetails.addEventListener(
        "collectionchange", updateValue);
    // Trigger load of OrderDetails
    order.getOrderDetails();
    // Clean up event listener
    contentItem.handleViewDispose(function () {
        parent.Children.removeEventListener(
            "collectionchange", updateValue);
    });
};
```

LightSwitch Client Side JavaScript Queries

It is possible to create client-side **JavaScript** queries. This allows you to retrieve data using a query without the need to create custom server-side code.

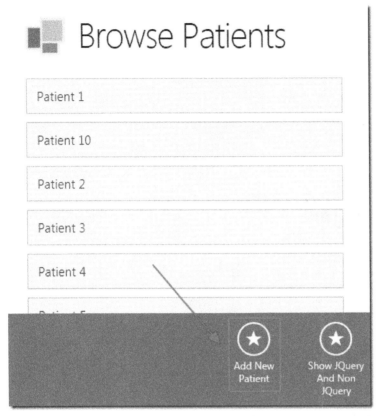

When we run the sample application, we can click the **Add New Patient** button to add a new record.

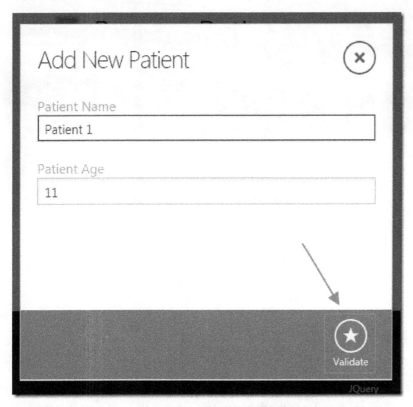

We can enter a **Name** and an **Age** and click the **Validate** button.

If a duplicate **Name** and **Age** are found, a validation message appears. We will have the option to navigate back.

*The key thing to note in this example is the values are validated against the entire database using a **client-side** query that runs **server-side**. If we had a large amount of records in the database, the query would still run fast because it does not require all the records to be transferred client-side to be searched.*

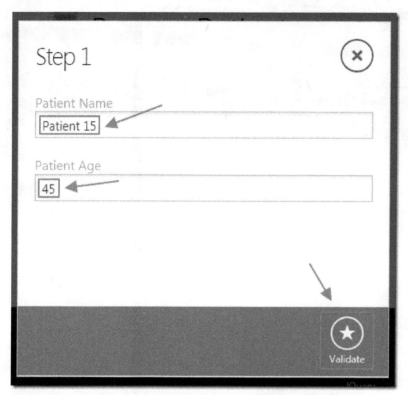

Step 1

Patient Name

Patient 15

Patient Age

45

Validate

We can change the information and click the **Validate** button again.

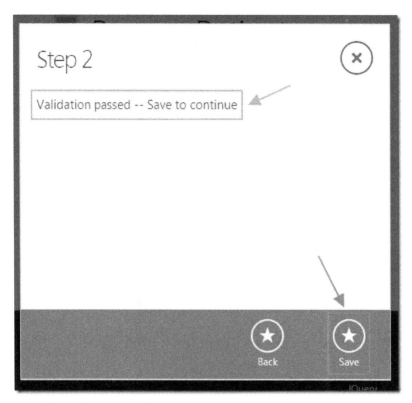

When the values pass validation, the **Save** button appears.

We can click the **Save** button to save the record.

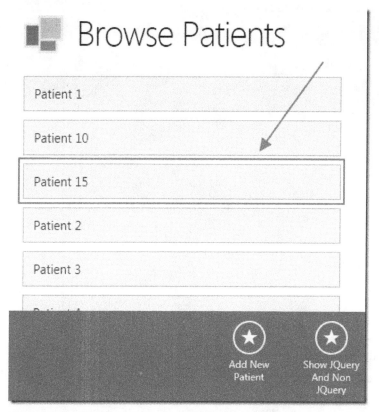

The record will be saved, and it will display in the list.

Creating the Example

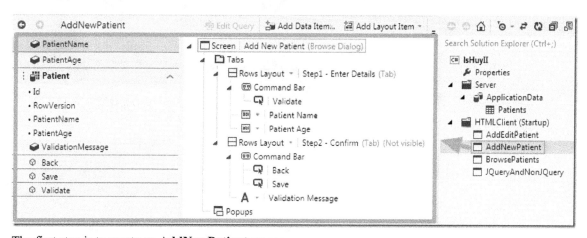

The first step is to create an **AddNewPatient** screen.

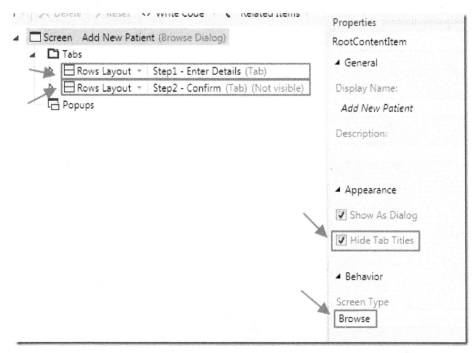

We create two **Tabs** and hide the second **Tab**.

We set the screen to hide the **Tab Titles**, and set the screen type to **Browse**, so the default **Save** button will not show.

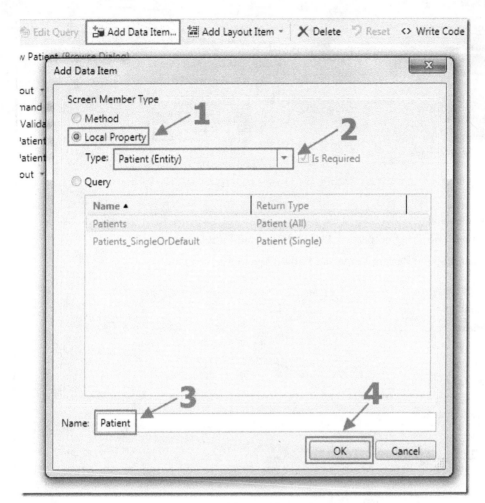

We use the **Add Data Item** button to add a **Patient** entity.

This entity will be used to hold the final record we are constructing with the wizard.

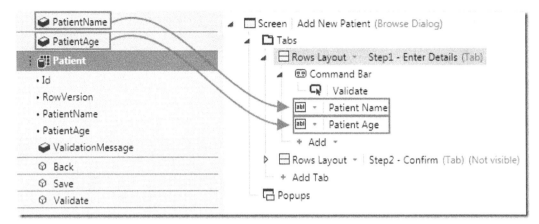

We also create two string properties, **PatientName** and **PatientAge**.

We drag and drop the **PatientName** and **PatientAge** to the first **Tab**.

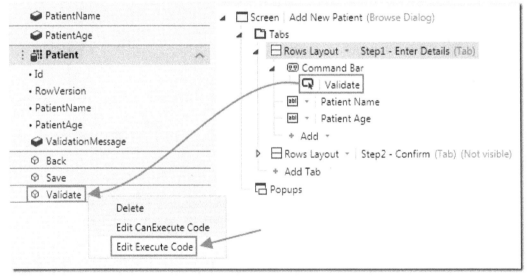

We also create a **Validate** button for the first **Tab** and use the following code for the method:

```
myapp.AddNewPatient.Validate_execute = function (screen) {
    // get the values entered
    var PatientName = screen.PatientName;
    var PatientAge = screen.PatientAge;
    // Always show step 2 at this point
    screen.showTab("Step2");
    screen.details.displayName = "Step 2";
    // Clear ValidationMessage
    screen.ValidationMessage = "";
    if (PatientName == null || PatientAge == null) {
        screen.ValidationMessage = "Both values are required -- Click Back and try again";
        // Hide the Save button
        var SaveButton = screen.findContentItem("Save");
        SaveButton.isVisible = false;
        // Stop processing
        return;
    }
    // Check to see if this is a duplicate -- construct a query
    var filter = "(PatientName eq " + msls._toODataString(PatientName, ":String") +
        ") and (PatientAge eq " + msls._toODataString(PatientAge, ":Int32") + ")";
    // Query the database
    myapp.activeDataWorkspace.ApplicationData
        .Patients
        .filter(filter)
        .execute()
        .then(function (result) {
            // Get the results of the query
            var currentPatient = result.results[0];
            // If there are any results show duplicate record error
            if (currentPatient != null && currentPatient != 'undefined') {
                screen.ValidationMessage = "Duplicate Found -- Click Back and try again";
                // Hide the Save button
                var SaveButton = screen.findContentItem("Save");
                SaveButton.isVisible = false;
            } else {
                // There is no duplication
                screen.ValidationMessage = "Validation passed -- Save to continue";
                // Show the Save button
                var SaveButton = screen.findContentItem("Save");
                SaveButton.isVisible = true;
            }
        }, function (error) {
            alert(error);
        });
};
```

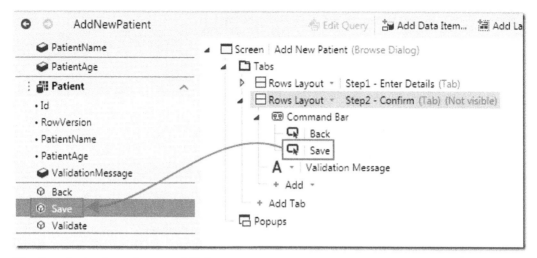

The **Save** button is on the second **Tab**.

We use the following code for the method called by the button:

```
myapp.AddNewPatient.Save_execute = function (screen) {
    // Get the values entered
    var PatientName = screen.PatientName;
    var PatientAge = screen.PatientAge;
    // Set the values for the entity
    screen.Patient.PatientName = PatientName;
    screen.Patient.PatientAge = PatientAge;
    // Save and close
    myapp.commitChanges();
};
```

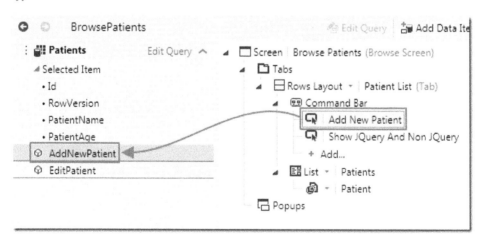

We open the **BrowsePatients** screen and create a button called **Add New Patient**.

We use the following code for the method called by the button:

```
myapp.BrowsePatients.AddNewPatient_execute = function (screen) {
    // Open the AddNewPatient Screen
    myapp.showAddNewPatient({
        beforeShown: function (addEditPatientScreen) {
            // Create new Patient here so that
            // discard will work.
            var newPatient = new myapp.Patient;
            addEditPatientScreen.Patient = newPatient;
        },
        afterClosed: function (AddNewPatientScreen, navigationAction) {
            // Refresh Patients
            screen.Patients.load();
        }
    });
};
```

Client-Side JavaScript API

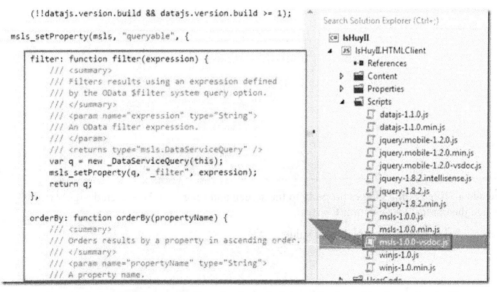

```
(!!datajs.version.build && datajs.version.build >= 1);

msls_setProperty(msls, "queryable", {

    filter: function filter(expression) {
        /// <summary>
        /// Filters results using an expression defined
        /// by the OData $filter system query option.
        /// </summary>
        /// <param name="expression" type="String">
        /// An OData filter expression.
        /// </param>
        /// <returns type="msls.DataServiceQuery" />
        var q = new _DataServiceQuery(this);
        msls_setProperty(q, "_filter", expression);
        return q;
    },

    orderBy: function orderBy(propertyName) {
        /// <summary>
        /// Orders results by a property in ascending order.
        /// </summary>
        /// <param name="propertyName" type="String">
        /// A property name.
```

The **API** methods for the *client-side* **JavaScript** queries can be found in the **vsdoc.js** file:

*Note: For more information on the **OData** commands to use in the "filter" expression, see:*
Filter System Query Option ($filter) *(http://bit.ly/14S42LF).*

Controls

The sample code for this section can be obtained at the links "Walk-thru Examples of Common Visual Studio LightSwitch JavaScript", and "HUY Volume II - Visual Studio LightSwitch Advanced JavaScript Examples" at http://lightswitchhelpwebsite.com/Downloads.aspx.

Use a JQuery Mobile Control

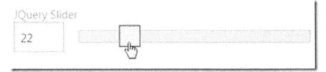

There are several **JQuery** controls that we can implement. In this example, we will implement the **JQuery** slider.

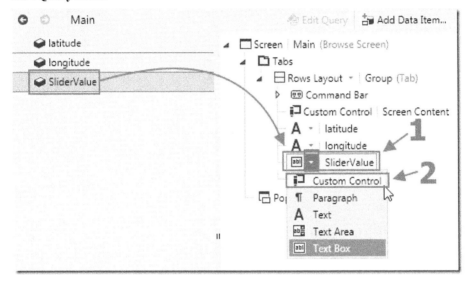

We add a **SliderValue** integer property to the screen and drag it to the screen designer and change the control to a **Custom Control**.

We could also bind to a normal table value.

In the **Properties** for the control, we select **Edit Render Code** and use the following code:

```
myapp.Main.SliderValue_render = function (element, contentItem) {
    createSlider(element, contentItem, 0, 100);
};
function createSlider(element, contentItem, min, max) {
    // Generate the input element.
    $(element).append('<input type="range" min="' + min +
        '" max="' + max + '" value="' + contentItem.value + '" />');
};
```

Prevent JQuery Mobile from Overriding Custom Controls

You can use the *data-role="none"* attribute to prevent the underlying **JQuery Mobile** framework from automatically augmenting and styling certain controls. This can be useful when the **JQuery Mobile** augmentation causes problems.

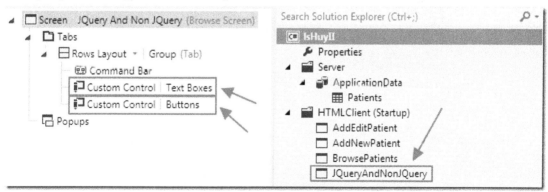

For this example, we create a page called **JQueryAndNonJQuery**.

We place two **Custom Controls** on the page, one for **Text Boxes** and one for **Buttons**.

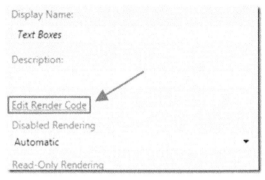

Display Name:

Text Boxes

Description:

Edit Render Code

Disabled Rendering

Automatic ▼

Read-Only Rendering

In the **Properties** for each control, we click the **Edit Render Code** link.

We use the following code for each control:

```
myapp.JQueryAndNonJQuery.TextBoxes_render = function (element, contentItem) {
    var $element = $(element);
    var $textbox1 = $('<input type="text" value="Normal Text Box" data-role="none"/>');
    var $textbox2 = $('<input type="text" value="JQuery Text Box"/>');
    $element.append($textbox1);
    $element.append($textbox2);
};
myapp.JQueryAndNonJQuery.Buttons_render = function (element, contentItem) {
    var $element = $(element);
    var $button1 = $('<input type="button" value="Normal Button" data-role="none"/>');
    var $button2 = $('<input type="button" value="JQuery Button" />');
    $element.append($button1);
    $element.append($button2);
};
```

When we run the project, we get the following output:

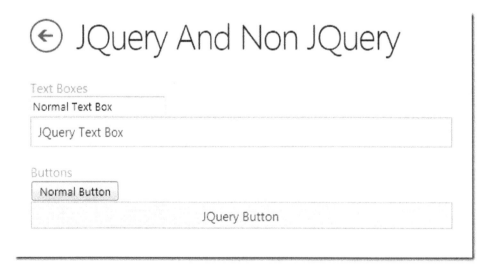

Theming

It is possible to alter the default theme of your **LightSwtch HTML** application.

The **Visual Studio LightSwitch HTML Client** uses **JQuery Mobile**, and it is compatible with http://jquerymobile.com/themeroller/.

The Application Before

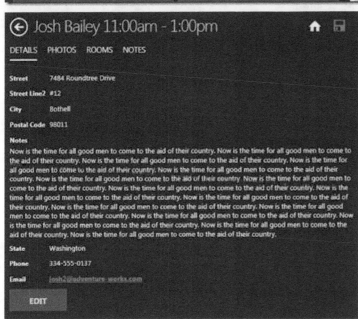

Get the Current Theme

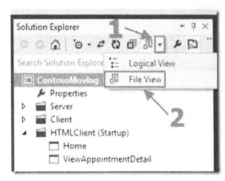

To get the current theme, we first switch to **File View**.

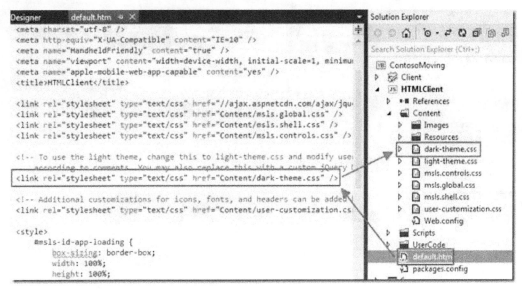

We open the **Default.htm** page and see it is using the theme in the **dark-theme.css** file. In your project, you may be using **light-theme.css**

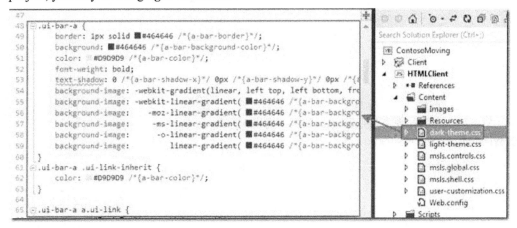

We open up the **.css** file and copy the contents.

Using ThemeRoller

To use *ThemeRoller*, go to http://jquerymobile.com/themeroller/.

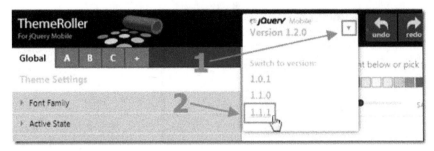

Switch to version **1.1.1** (or whatever version of **JQuery Mobile** is in the **Default.htm** file of the **LightSwitch** website).

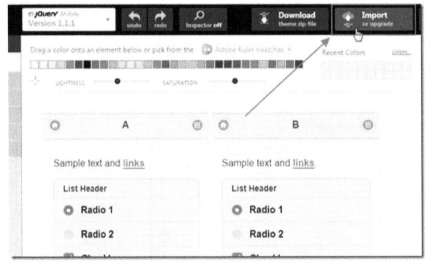

Next, click on the **Import** button.

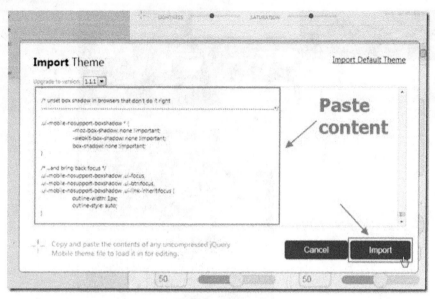

Paste in the contents of the **.css** file and click **Import**.

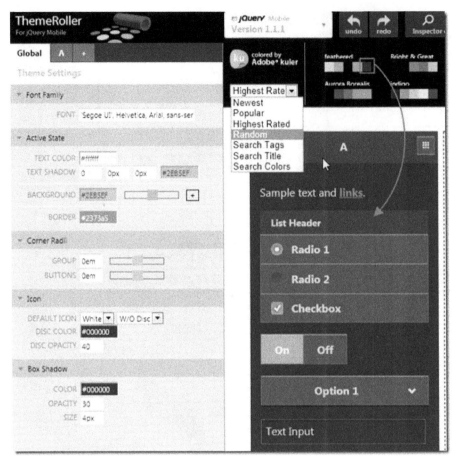

You can now design the theme. Drag the little color blocks and drop them on the mockup of the sample application.

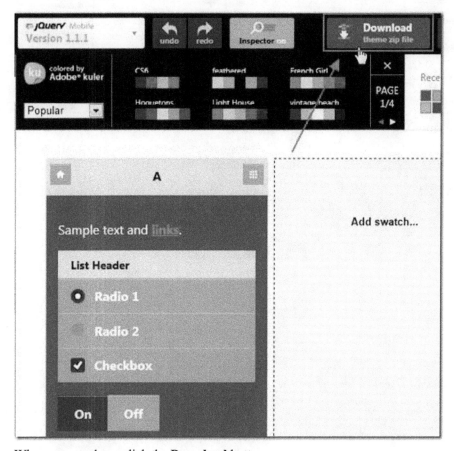

When you are done, click the **Download** button.

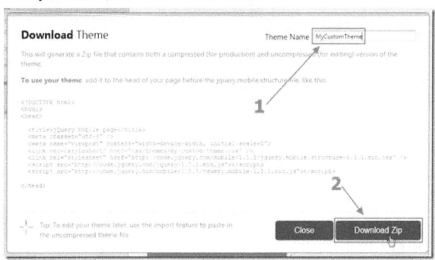

Give the theme a name and click the **Download Zip** button.

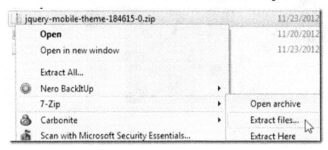

Download the .zip file and *un-zip* it.

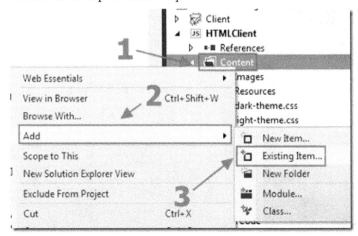

Right-click on the **Content** folder and select **Add** then **Existing Item**.

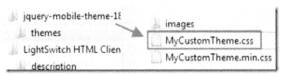

Select the theme.

```
<!-- To use the light theme, change this to light-theme.css and modify user-customization.css
     according to comments. You may also replace this with a custom jquery Mobile theme. -->
<link rel="stylesheet" type="text/css" href="Content/MyCustomTheme.css" />

<!-- Additional customizations for icons, fonts, and headers can be added here. -->
<link rel="stylesheet" type="text/css" href="Content/user-customization.css"/>
```

Update the **default.html** file to point to the new theme.

The Application After

When we run the application, it has a new theme:

Home

Upcoming Appointments

Fri, Nov 23rd, 11:00-1:00pm Josh Bailey - 334-555-0137	**Mon, Nov 26th, 9:00-11:00am** Stig Panduro - 818-555-0171
Sat, Dec 1st, 12:00-2:00pm Russell King - 1 900 555-0198	**Wed, Dec 5th, 10:00-12:00pm** Ioanna Yuan - 226-555-0146
Sun, Dec 9th, 9:00-11:00am	**Mon, Dec 17th, 8:00-10:00am**

 Josh Bailey 11:00am - 1:00pm

DETAILS   PHOTOS   ROOMS   NOTES

Street	7484 Roundtree Drive
Street Line2	#12
City	Bothell
Postal Code	98011

Notes

Now is the time for all good men to come to the aid of their country. Now is the time for all good men to come to the aid of their country. Now is the time for all good men to come to the aid of their country. Now is the time for all good men to come to the aid of their country. Now is the time for all good men to come to the aid of their country. Now is the time for all good men to come to the aid of their country. Now is the time for all good men to come to the aid of their country. Now is the time for all good men to come to the aid of their country. Now is the time for all good men to come to the aid of their country. Now is the time for all good men to come to the aid of their country. Now is the time for all good men to come to the aid of their country. Now is the time for all good men to come to the aid of their country. Now is the time for all good men to come to the aid of their country.

State	Washington
Phone	334-555-0137
Email	josh2@adventure-works.com

EDIT

Updating the LightSwitch JavaScript Runtime

This is a step-by-step guide to updating the **LightSwitch JavaScript Runtime**. Depending on the version of **JQuery Mobile** you have installed, you may need to do this to create applications in the following sections.

Make a **New Project**.

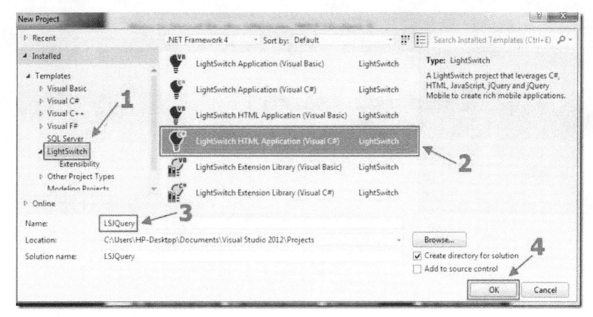

Create the project.

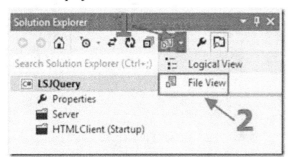

Switch to **File View**.

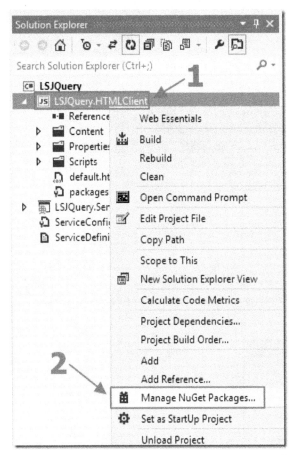

Right-click on the **HTMLClient** project and select **Manage NuGet Packages**.

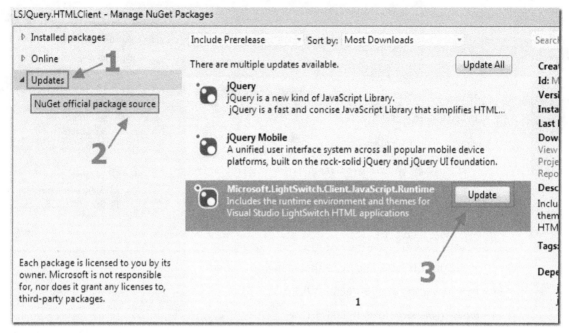

Select **Updates**, then **NuGet official package source**.

Click on the **Microsoft.LightSwitch.Client.JavaScript.Runtime** and then click the **Update** button.

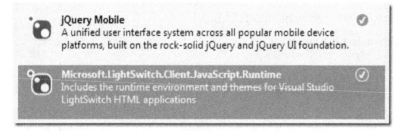

The **Runtime** will update and **JQuery Mobile** will also be updated.

```
<!DOCTYPE HTML>
<html>
<head>
    <meta charset="utf-8" />
    <meta http-equiv="X-UA-Compatible" content="IE=10" />
    <meta name="HandheldFriendly" content="true" />
    <meta name="viewport" content="width=device-width, initial-:
    <meta name="apple-mobile-web-app-capable" content="yes" />
    <title>LSJQuery</title>

    <script type="text/javascript">
        // Work around viewport sizing issue in IE 10 on Window:
        if (navigator.userAgent.match(/IEMobile\/10\.0/)) {
            document.writeln("<style>@-ms-viewport { width: aut(
        }
    </script>

    <!-- Change light-theme.css and msls-light.css to dark-them(
        dark theme. Alternatively. you may replace light-them(
```

- LSJQuery
- LSJQuery.HTMLClient
  - References
  - Content
  - Properties
  - Scripts
  - default.htm
  - packages.config
- LSJQuery.Server
  - ServiceConfiguration.cscfg
  - ServiceDefinition.csdef

Open the **default.htm** file, and make the following changes:

- *light-theme.css* to light-theme-**1.0.1**.css

- *mlsls-light.css* to msls-light-**1.0.1**.css

- *jquery.mobile.structure-1.2.0.min.css* to jquery.mobile.structure-**1.3.0**.min.css

- *msls-1.0.0.min.css* to msls-**1.0.1**.min.css

- *jquery-1.8.2.min.js* to jquery-**1.9.1**.min.js

- *jquery.mobile-1.2.0.min.js* to jquery.mobile-**1.3.0**.min.js

- *msls-1.0.0.min.js* to msls-**1.0.1**.min.js

To update **LightSwitch** to versions of **JQuery** that are not available as a **NuGet** package, download the latest **JQuery .js** and **.css** files from the **JQuery Mobile site**, http://jquerymobile.com/download/.

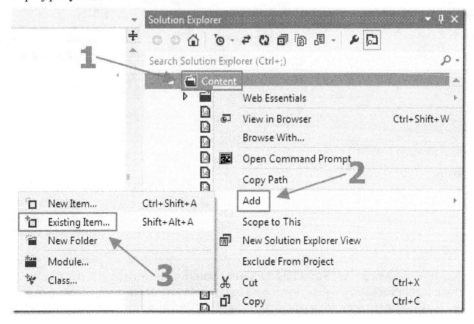

Use **Add/Existing Item** to add the files to their proper folders (**.css** goes in the **Content** folder, and **.js** goes in the **Scripts** folder).

```
<link rel="stylesheet" type="text/css" href="Content/jquery.mobile.structure-1.3.1.min.css" />
<link rel="stylesheet" type="text/css" href="Content/msls-1.0.1.min.css" />
<link rel="stylesheet" type="text/css" href="Content/CustomButtonStylesheet.css" />

<!-- Default font, header, and icon styles can be overriden in user-customization.css -->
<link rel="stylesheet" type="text/css" href="Content/user-customization.css" />
</head>
<body>
    <div id="msls-id-app-loading" class="ui-body-a msls-layout-ignore">
        <div class="msls-app-loading-img"></div>
        <span class="ui-icon ui-icon-loading"></span>
        <div class="ui-bottom-load">
            <div>LSJQuery</div>
        </div>
    </div>

    <script type="text/javascript" src="//ajax.aspnetcdn.com/ajax/globalize/0.1.1/globalize.min.js"></script
    <script type="text/javascript" src="Scripts/winjs-1.0.min.js"></script>
    <script type="text/javascript" src="Scripts/jquery-1.9.1.min.js"></script>
    <script type="text/javascript" src="Scripts/jquery.mobile-1.3.1.min.js"></script>
    <script type="text/javascript" src="Scripts/datajs-1.1.0.min.js"></script>
```

Open the **default.htm** page and update the references.

LightSwitch HTML for the Desktop

The sample code for this section can be obtained at the link "LightSwitch HTML Client for The Desktop Web Browser" at http://lightswitchhelpwebsite.com/Downloads.aspx.

One objection many developers have about using **Visual Studio LightSwitch HTML Client** for their projects is that they feel they need *normal* web pages. To many developers, **LightSwitch HTML** pages look odd when viewed in a normal desktop web browser.

With the release of **JQuery Mobile 1.3.1**, **JQuery Mobile** has moved from *Mobile* to *Mobile first*. Meaning, **JQuery Mobile** still primarily creates mobile web applications, but it now has controls that will work well for both desktop and mobile applications.

JQuery Mobile 1.3.1 brings a number of features that allow you to create applications that look great on both desktop web browsers and mobile web browsers. One of the best is the **Reflow table** that will be explored here.

The **Reflow table** displays data in a desktop web browser like any normal data grid, yet it will dynamically pivot the table when the screen becomes smaller, rather than just squeezing the table smaller. A user can easily view and navigate the table on any sized device.

Update the LightSwitch JavaScript Runtime

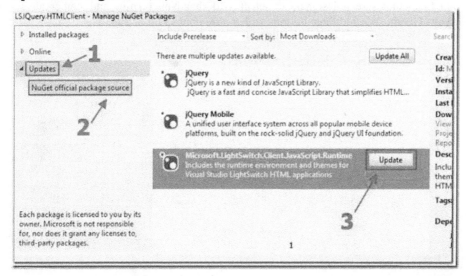

First, follow the directions in the earlier section to update the **Visual Studio LightSwitch Client JavaScript Runtime**. Also, follow the directions to update it to **JQuery Mobile 1.3.1** (or higher).

The Built-in Screen Adaption Features

LightSwitch has built-in features that allow you to easily create screens that will adapt to any screen size. The most powerful technique is using *columns* that will automatically collapse its containing elements underneath each other when the screen size becomes smaller.

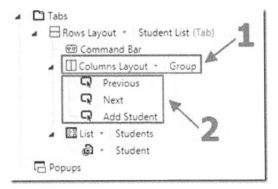

To demonstrate this, in the screen designer, we select **Add**, then **New Group**, and then create a **Columns Layout Group**. We add three buttons with a *minimum width* of **200**.

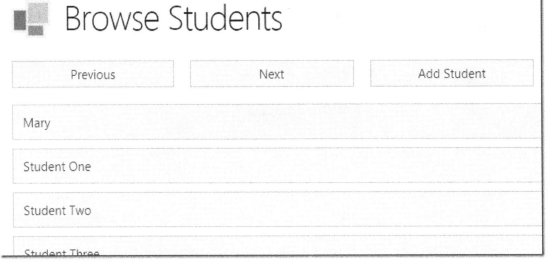

When we run the application, the buttons will be on the same line when we have a wide screen.

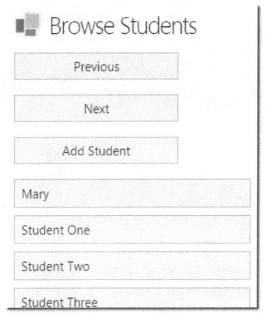

They will stack on top of each other when we have a smaller one.

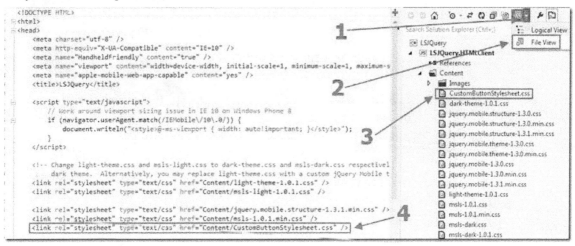

We can style the buttons by switching to **File View**, adding a custom **.css** style, and then adding a reference to that style in the **default.htm** page.

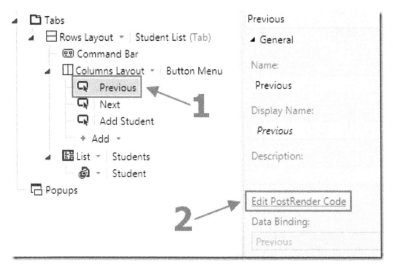

We then select the **Edit PostRender Code** link for each button, and add a style to each button:

```
myapp.BrowseStudents.Previous_postRender = function (element, contentItem) {
    var PreviousButtonOutside = $(element);
    var PreviousButtonInside = $(element).children();
    PreviousButtonOutside.addClass("gray");
    PreviousButtonInside.addClass("orange");
};
myapp.BrowseStudents.Next_postRender = function (element, contentItem) {
    var NextButtonOutside = $(element);
    var NextButtonInside = $(element).children();
    NextButtonOutside.addClass("gray");
    NextButtonInside.addClass("blue");
};
myapp.BrowseStudents.AddStudent_postRender = function (element, contentItem) {
    var AddStudentButtonOutside = $(element);
    var AddStudentButtonInside = $(element).children();
    AddStudentButtonOutside.addClass("gray");
    AddStudentButtonInside.addClass("green");
};
```

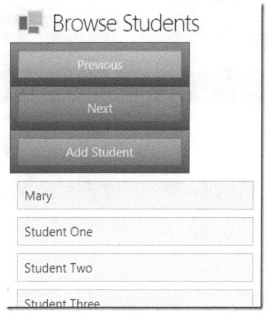

When we run the application, the buttons look more attractive.

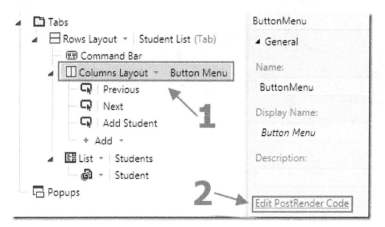

We can also select the group control, and select the **Edit PostRender Code** link for it.

Use the following:

```
myapp.BrowseStudents.ButtonMenu_postRender = function (element, contentItem) {
    var MenuElementElementInside = $(element);
    MenuElementElementInside.css({
        "position": "relative",
        "float": "right"
    });
};
```

When the screen is wider, the buttons will now be right justified.

Implementing the JQuery Reflow Table

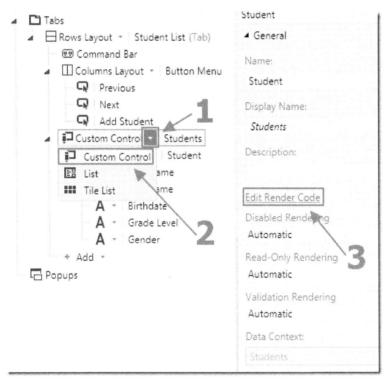

To implement the **JQuery Reflow Table**, we switch the **Student List** to a **Custom Control**.

We then select the **Edit Render Code** link for the control.

We use the following code:

```javascript
var intCurrentItem = 0;
var intPageSize = 5;
var StudentTable;



myapp.BrowseStudents.StudentsGrid_render = function (element, contentItem) {
    // clear the element
    element.innerHTML = "";
    // Create a table
    var strTable = "<table id='studentTable' class='ui-responsive table-stroke'";
    strTable = strTable + " data-role='table' data-mode='reflow'></table>";
    StudentTable = $(strTable);
    // Create thead
    var theadTemplate = $("<thead></thead>");
    theadTemplate.appendTo($(StudentTable));
    // Create tableRow
    var tablerowTemplate = $("<tr class='ui-bar-d'></tr>");
    tablerowTemplate.appendTo($(theadTemplate));
    // Crate Columns
    var Column1Template = $("<th data-priority='6'>ID</th>");
    Column1Template.appendTo($(tablerowTemplate));
    var Column2Template = $("<th data-priority='1'>First Name</th>");
    Column2Template.appendTo($(tablerowTemplate));
    var Column3Template = $("<th data-priority='2'>Last Name</th>");
    Column3Template.appendTo($(tablerowTemplate));
    var Column4Template = $("<th data-priority='3'>Birthdate</th>");
    Column4Template.appendTo($(tablerowTemplate));
    var Column5Template = $("<th data-priority='4'>Grade Level</th>");
    Column5Template.appendTo($(tablerowTemplate));
    var Column6Template = $("<th data-priority='5'>Gender</th>");
    Column6Template.appendTo($(tablerowTemplate));
    // Create tableBody
    var tablebodyTemplate = $("<tbody></tbody>");
    tablebodyTemplate.appendTo($(StudentTable));
    // Complete the element
    StudentTable.appendTo($(element));
    // Function to show items
    // This is required because the removeEventListener
    // requires the same instance of the handler to be able to remove it
    function onVisualCollectionLoaded() {
        // Show the data in the JQuery reflow table
        showItems(intCurrentItem, intPageSize, contentItem.screen);
    }
    // Show Data
    var visualCollection = contentItem.value;
    // Do we have data?
    if (visualCollection.isLoaded) {
        // Load the data
        onVisualCollectionLoaded();
    } else {
        // Create a addChangeListener that will fire when the data is loaded
        visualCollection.addChangeListener("isLoaded", onVisualCollectionLoaded);
        // Load the data
        visualCollection.load();
    }
    // Clean up addChangeListener when screen is closed.
    contentItem.handleViewDispose(function () {
        // Remove the isLoaded change listener
        visualCollection.removeChangeListener(
            "isLoaded", onPropertyChanged);
    });
};
```

The code above calls the following function to show the data in the grid:

```
function showItems(start, end, screen) {
    // Remove existing rows
    StudentTable.find("tr:gt(0)").remove();
    $.each(screen.Students.data, function (i, student) {
        if (i >= start && i < end) {
            // Create tableRow
            var tablecontentrowTemplate = $("<tr></tr>");
            tablecontentrowTemplate.appendTo($(StudentTable));
            // Set the row iD
            tablecontentrowTemplate.id = student.Id;
            // Create ID
            var IdTemplate = $("<th>" + student.Id + "</th>");
            IdTemplate.appendTo($(tablecontentrowTemplate));
            // Create FirstName
            var FirstNameTemplate = $("<td>").text(student.FirstName);
            FirstNameTemplate.appendTo($(tablecontentrowTemplate));
            // Create LastName
            var LastNameTemplate = $("<td>").text(student.LastName);
            LastNameTemplate.appendTo($(tablecontentrowTemplate));
            // Create Birthdate
            var dtBirthdate = new Date(student.Birthdate);
            var formattedBirthDate =
                ((dtBirthdate.getMonth() + 1) + "/" + dtBirthdate.getDate() + "/" + dtBirthdate.getFullYear());
            var BirthdateTemplate = $("<td>" + formattedBirthDate + "</td>");
            BirthdateTemplate.appendTo($(tablecontentrowTemplate));
            // Create GradeLevel
            var GradeLevelTemplate = $("<td>" + student.GradeLevel + "</td>");
            GradeLevelTemplate.appendTo($(tablecontentrowTemplate));
            // Create Gender
            var GenderTemplate = $("<td>").text(student.Gender);
            GenderTemplate.appendTo($(tablecontentrowTemplate));
            // Change mouse curser to hand
            $(tablecontentrowTemplate).css('cursor', 'pointer');
            // Add click event
            $(tablecontentrowTemplate).click(function () {
                // Id of selected Student
                var selectedStudentID = tablecontentrowTemplate.id;
                // Get the selected Student
                myapp.activeDataWorkspace.ApplicationData.Students_SingleOrDefault(selectedStudentID)
                    .execute()
                    .then(function (result) {
                    // Set the selected Student
                    screen.Students.selectedItem = result.results[0];
                    // Show selected Student in Edit screen
                    myapp.showAddEditStudent(screen.Students.selectedItem,{
                        afterClosed: function (addEditScreen, navigationAction) {
                            // If the user commits a change,
                            // show the new Student in Browse Screen.
                            if (navigationAction === msls.NavigateBackAction.commit) {
                                // Update the Grid//
                                showItems(intCurrentItem, intCurrentItem + intPageSize, screen);
                            }
                        }
                    });
                });
            });
        };
    });
    // Refresh the StudentTable
    StudentTable.table("refresh");
};
```

To make the table show the full width, we open the *Content/jquery.mobile.theme-1.3.1.css* file and alter the *.ui-table-reflow.ui-responsive* tag to:

```
.ui-table-reflow.ui-responsive {
    display: table;
}
```

Next, we run the application.

Browse Students

| | Previous | | Next | | Add Student |

ID	First Name	Last Name	Birthdate	Grade Level	Gender
2	Mary	Jones	7/24/2005	11	F
4	Student One	One	8/20/2006	12	M
5	Student Two	Two	11/27/2006	8	F
6	Student Three	Three	1/24/2007	12	M
7	Student Four	Four	11/22/2006	11	F

When the window is wide, the table shows each row of data on its own line.

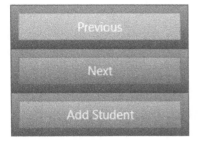

Browse Students

Previous	
Next	
Add Student	

ID	2
First Name	Mary
Last Name	Jones
Birthdate	7/24/2005
Grade Level	11
Gender	F

ID	4
First Name	Student One
Last Name	One
Birthdate	8/20/2006

When the screen is smaller, it uses multiple lines to clearly show each row of data.

Paging

Normally, **LightSwitch** provides paging for the data. When you implement a control that completely renders the data, you must implement the code to handle paging.

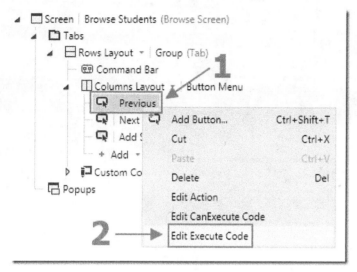

In the screen designer, we *right-click* on the **Previous** button and select **Edit Execute Code**.

We use the following code:

```
myapp.BrowseStudents.Previous_Tap_execute = function (screen) {
    // Only move back if we are not on the first record
    if (intCurrentItem > 0) {
        // Move the current record back by the page size
        intCurrentItem = intCurrentItem - intPageSize;
        showItems(intCurrentItem, intCurrentItem + intPageSize, screen);
    }
};
```

We do the same for the **Next** button and use the following code:

```
myapp.BrowseStudents.Next_Tap_execute = function (screen) {
    // We always try to move forward at this point
    // We may move back (later in this method)
    // If we are moving too far forward
    intCurrentItem = intCurrentItem + intPageSize;
    // If we are trying to move to a record
    // that is higher than all the records we have
    // try to load more records
    if (intCurrentItem + intPageSize >= screen.Students.count) {
        // See if we can load more records
        if (screen.Students.canLoadMore) {
            // We can load more records -- load them
            screen.Students.loadMore().then(function (result) {
                showItems(intCurrentItem, intCurrentItem + intPageSize, screen);
            });
        } else {
            // If we are here then we have no more records to load
            // See if we have moved too far forward
            if (intCurrentItem >= screen.Students.count) {
                //We have moved too far forward so move back
                intCurrentItem = intCurrentItem - intPageSize;
            }
            showItems(intCurrentItem, intCurrentItem + intPageSize, screen);
        }
    } else {
        // We are trying to show records that we already have loaded
        // Show them
        showItems(intCurrentItem, intCurrentItem + intPageSize, screen);
    }
};
```

Editing

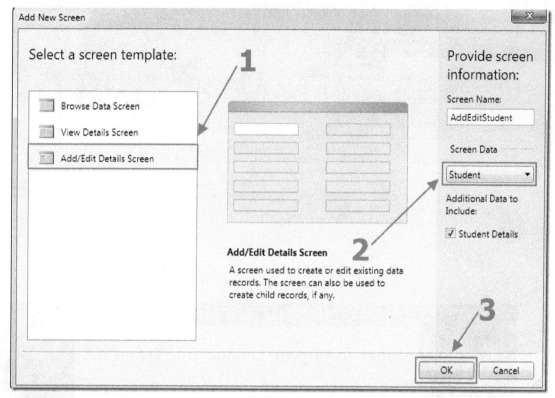

To allow a record to be edited, we first create a normal **Add/Edit Details** screen for the entity in **LightSwitch**.

LightSwitch will automatically create a **showAddEditStudent** method that will allow us to programmatically open this screen.

We then add the following code to the **showItems** method in the screen that displays the **Reflow** table:

```
// Add click event
$(tablecontentrowTemplate).click(function () {
    // Id of selected Student
    var selectedStudentID = tablecontentrowTemplate.id;
    // Get the selected Student
    myapp.activeDataWorkspace.ApplicationData.Students_SingleOrDefault(selectedStudentID)
        .execute()
        .then(function (result) {
        // Set the selected Student
        screen.Students.selectedItem = result.results[0];
        // Show selected Student in Edit screen
        myapp.showAddEditStudent(screen.Students.selectedItem,{
            afterClosed: function (addEditScreen, navigationAction) {
                // If the user commits a change,
                // show the new Student in Browse Screen.
                if (navigationAction === msls.NavigateBackAction.commit) {
                    // Update the Grid//
                    showItems(intCurrentItem, intCurrentItem + intPageSize, screen);
                }
            }
        });
    });
});
```

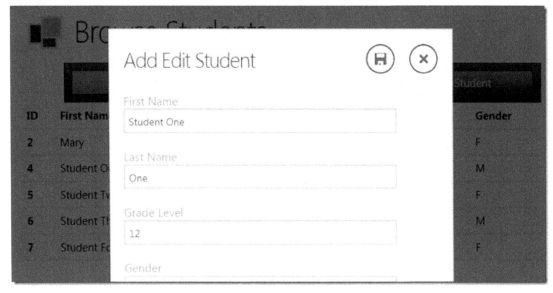

When we click on a row in the table, the row will come up in the edit screen.

Adding Records

To add a record, the following code is used:

```
myapp.BrowseStudents.AddStudent_Tap_execute = function (screen) {
    myapp.showAddEditStudent(null, {
        beforeShown: function (addEditScreen) {
            // Create new Student here so that
            // discard will work.
            var newStudent = new myapp.Student();
            addEditScreen.Student = newStudent;
        },
        afterClosed: function (addEditScreen, navigationAction) {
            // If the user commits the change,
            // show the new Student in Browse Screen.
            if (navigationAction === msls.NavigateBackAction.commit) {
                // Update the Grid//
                showItems(intCurrentItem, intCurrentItem + intPageSize, screen);
            }
        }
    });
};
```

About The Author

 Michael Washington is an ASP.NET, C#, and Visual Basic programmer. He has extensive knowledge in process improvement, billing systems, and student information systems. He is a Microsoft MVP. He has a son, Zachary, and resides in Los Angeles with his wife, Valerie.

He has written nearly 100 Visual Studio LightSwitch tutorials at: http://lightswitchhelpwebsite.com/Blog.aspx.

He is the author of four previous books:

- **OData And Visual Studio LightSwitch** (LightSwitchHelpWebsite.com)
- **Creating Visual Studio LightSwitch Custom Controls (Beginner to Intermediate)** (LightSwitchHelpWebsite.com)
- **Building Websites with VB.NET and DotNetNuke 4** (Packt Publishing)
- **Building Websites with DotNetNuke 5** (Packt Publishing)